GOOGLE PROFESSIONAL CLOUD ARCHITECT

Cloud Architect Exam Practice Questions & Actual Test Dumps: Pass For Sure Exam Prep Material with 100+ Questions & Explanations

By

Jason Hoffman

Edition 2020

ISBN:

Disclaimer

The content of this book has been checked and compiled with great care. For the completeness, correctness and topicality of the contents however no guarantee or guarantee can be taken over. The content of this book represents the personal experience and opinion of the author and is for entertainment purposes only. The content should not be confused with medical help.

There will be no legal responsibility or liability for damages resulting from counterproductive exercise or errors by the reader. No guarantee can be given for success. The author therefore assumes no responsibility for the non-achievement of the goals described in the book.

Table of Contents

Disclaimer 3

CHAPTER ONE - GOOGLE CERTIFIED PROFESSIONAL ARCHITECT OVERVIEW 7

CHAPTER TWO - ARCHITECTING WITH GOOGLE COMPUTER ENGINE 23

CHAPTER THREE - PREPARATION FOR THE PROFESSIONAL CLOUD ARCHITECT EXAM 33

CHAPTER FOUR - GETTING STARTED WITH GOOGLE KUBERNETES ENGINE 47

CHAPTER FIVE- DESIGNING AND PLANNING A CLOUD SOLUTION ARCHITECTURE 68

CHAPTER SIX - MANAGING AND PROVIDING THE CLOUD SOLUTION INFRASTRUCTURE 84

CHAPTER SEVEN - SECURITY DESIGN AND COMPLIANCE FOR CLOUD SOLUTION 101

CHAPTER EIGHT- HOW TO ENSURE SOLUTION AND OPERATION RELIABILITY OF CLOUD ARCHITECTURE 119

CHAPTER NINE- EXAM GUIDE 133

CHAPTER TEN - PROFESSIONAL CLOUD ARCHITECT EXAM 154

CHAPTER ELEVEN - CONCLUSION 160

CONCLUSION/ APPRECIATION 172

CHAPTER ONE - GOOGLE CERTIFIED PROFESSIONAL ARCHITECT OVERVIEW

Introduction

Google certified professional Architecture is a program for individuals who have an interest in Google cloud computing architecture or cloud computing services. They must undergo the rigorous assessment of this program to have the certification needed and attain the name or become a Google cloud certified professional architect on Google cloud platform.

Individuals take up this program for boosting their careers, depending on their areas of interest. Google cloud platforms offer different certification programs or courses for individuals interested or Information Technology expertise. Programs such as:

1. Professional Data Engineer: This program enables the abilities in developing data engineering, building data collection, data processing including design and machine learning on Google cloud platform(GCP)

2. Professional Cloud Developer: This program promotes in delivering full-stack knowledge and skills in the scalable application of the Google cloud platform model.

3. Professional Cloud Security Engineering: This course is exclusively meant for future security engineers. They have the intention to secure the cloud infrastructure of the company using the Google cloud's platform security tools.

4. Professional Cloud Architects: This program helps in acquiring knowledge about complex cloud computing services in Google cloud platforms and are among the highest-paid professionals in the Google cloud platform profession.

5. Professional Collaboration Engineers: This is a course that is exclusively meant for individuals targeting to become a G-suite specialist in the later stage.

6. Professional Cloud Network Engineer: This program helps in designing, implementing and managing the architecture in the Google cloud platform model.

All of these and more are the numerous programs offered by Google as our world turn virtual by the day. All these certifications validate once expertise and show ones ability to transform businesses with Google cloud technology, but that's for that.

Google Certified Professional Architecture as a course, oversees the transfer of knowledge and understanding of cloud computing services, cloud computing architecture and its infrastructures. This certification program provides Google cloud professionals a way to demonstrate their skills.

Google is an art or practice of designing and building of structures and components, even sub-components which are connected and deliver to an online platform. Components that makeup clouds like hardware, virtual resources, management container, automation middleware and more are connected to create a cloud computing environment. So the integrating of the distinct technologies to create an information technology environment or cloud computing environment.

In cloud architecture, tools are required to create such, and these tools are known as **Cloud Infrastructure**.

Cloud architects are responsible for managing the cloud architecture in an organization, especially as cloud technologies grow increasingly complex. For a better understanding of what this Google cloud architecture is all about, and its components, the explanation of the reoccurring words or rather key words will be explained. Words like cloud, cloud computing services, cloud computing architecture and Google cloud platforms.

CLOUD

Cloud is a set of tools that help developers spend less time managing and more time creating.

What do I mean? Cloud are referred to as servers that are

accessed over the internet, and the software and databases that run on those servers. Its also a platform that hosts a pool of computing resources over the internet as a convenient, on-demand utility to be rented on a pay-as-you-go basis. All clouds are virtualized data centres made up of computation and storage resources.

However, this has not always been the case. It all started with what we call '**on-premise**' which is a software that is installed and runs on computers on the premises of the person or organization using the software. Due to the fact it's within a limited environment, its server is limited too. For example, an organization has a computer with a single server and probably five users and the next day, there's a thousand user because a single server is being used it will crash. Then **scaling** came into play, which was seen to be a temporary remedy to on-premise. Scaling however involved the use of more than one computer, tons of coding and quite a bit of data sharing between the computers involved to link it. Scaling, therefore, helped to serve and reach more users than the on-premise software.

However, this scaling seems to be time and resource exhausting.

Then **time sharing** came about, which involved the sharing of computing resources among many users at the same time using multi-programming and multi-tasking.

With continued usage and passing of time, companies who owned and managed direct access to the sharing decided to add services like Infrastructure as a Service(IaaS), Platform as a Service(PaaS), Software as a Service(SaaS) which led to Cloud services as we know it today. Clouds are everywhere, and it influences everyday life, from our emails, shopping apps, to banking transactions, all use the cloud one way or another. Clouds have different models they offer based on diverse, unique business models. We have models such as;

- **Public cloud:** this is a cloud whose resources are shared by multiple customers. Each customer that procures the services of the cloud is known as a tenant. A public cloud can have numerous tenants sharing the same resources and services.
- **Private cloud:** here, the entire cloud is reserved for one tenant. As a tenant, you can customize the cloud according to your demand. You can also be connected to a private cloud by the use of either a private LAN or over the internet.
- **Hybrid cloud:** as the name implies, a hybrid cloud is a combination of public and private cloud providing the best of both worlds. With the hybrid cloud, when any of the resources on the private cloud are entirely occupied and needs to be increased, extra resources are borrowed from the public cloud, and this occurrence is called cloud bursting. Hybrid cloud gives you room to host a few of your applications on a public cloud and other crucial ones on a private cloud. It provides you with cost and resource savings according to your needs.

Google cloud platform

Google cloud platform is a public cloud-based machine which delivers services to customers on as you go basis. This platform allows business businesses to rent the software services and servers of Google themselves, instead of paying very hefty sum on-premise local servers. One can use Google enterprise suite of services and their immense computing power.

Cloud Computing Service

The term cloud computing service comprises all the services which are hosted over a cloud. Hence, cloud computing is the utilization of services such as storage, applications, and servers over the cloud.

Most organizations go to cloud services to reduce their investment in infrastructure costs, maintenance costs, and ensuring the availability of resources round the clock. Cloud computing is, therefore, a more efficient and cost-effective solution than traditional data centres. With all these, we see how efficient cloud computing service is, and this is due to its architectural framework, which is cloud computing architecture.

Cloud Computing Architecture

Cloud Computing architecture can be said to be as the different components and subcomponents that have been designed in terms of application, software capacities, databases, and so many more to maximize the function of cloud resources in other to provide long-lasting business solutions. Cloud Computing architecture is made up of three fundamental components, which include; Front-end platform, Back-end platform and cloud-based delivery.

Front-end Platform: front-end platform infrastructure includes everything that the end-user can interact with; it is a broader collection of different sub-components that together offer the user interface. The Front-end cloud architecture forms an essential part of how end-users connect to cloud computing architecture. This Front-end architecture includes components like; local network, web applications and web browsers. Specific components comprise the main front-end cloud architecture. Components such as;

User interface: this component refers to all of the elements that the end-user accesses to send request or perform any task on the cloud. Some of the popular cloud-based user interfaces include; g-mail and Google documents

Client system or network: this is a critical part of the front end cloud architecture. This client system or network refers to the hardware at the end-users end. It can be any input device or PC. When it comes to Google computing architecture, the client-side system doesn't require extraordinary abilities to process the heavy load. The cloud can store the entire massive data and also process it.

Software

The software component in the front end architecture is the software that operates on the user's side. The software component in the front-end architecture makes up the client-end applications or browsers.

Back-end

On the other hand, the back end is the "cloud" part of computing architecture, comprising all the resources required to deliver cloud-computing services. A systems back end can be made up of several bare metal servers, data storage facilities, virtual machines, a security mechanism and services, all built-in conformance with a deployment model, and altogether responsible for providing a service. The back end architecture must support the front-end platform. It consists of the hardware and storage components, and they are both located on a remote server. It is the function of the cloud service provider to oversee and manage the back-end cloud platform. Typically, the back end cloud architecture should usually be robust because it contains the entire infrastructure on the cloud.

The prime of the back-end cloud architecture are:

Storage: the data of a cloud application reside in cloud storage. Different cloud service providers offer different data storage; one thing they have in common is a reserved section for cloud storage. Example of storages are; hard-drives, solid-state drive etc. The hard drives in the server bays form storage in the cloud back-end architecture and especially in the cloud computing system, the software partitions, the drives as per the needs of the OS in the cloud to run multiple services.

Application: This application is a substantial aspect of the back-end architecture. It entails the user interface that the back-end platform provides the end-users with, to send queries. This part of the back-end takes care of the clients' request and requirements.

Infrastructure: this refers to the systems that direct all the cloud software services. This workload will always determine the infrastructure model. It includes; central processing unit(CPU), motherboard, graphics processing unit(GPU), accelerator cards, etc.

Management: the management software allocates specific resources to specific tasks and responsibilities for the flawless functioning of any cloud environment in technical terms, management is the 'middleware', and it coordinates between the front-end and back-end architecture in a cloud computing system.

Security: security is an integral and crucial part of cloud computing infrastructure. We create security infrastructure by keeping the debugging in mind. In case of any issue, debugging should be easy. Regular storage is the first thing to do to make security guaranteed. After that, you can affect virtual firewalls and other necessary elements that are critical in cloud security architecture.

Internet:

The internet is an avenue through which front end and back end platforms can interact and communicate with each other.

Service: the whole back-end cloud architecture receives utility from this essential aspect of the back-end cloud architecture. It is the function of the service to manage every task that operates on the cloud computing architecture. Some of the cloud services include web services, storage and app development environment. It is necessary also to mention that service can carry out a vast range of functions on the cloud run-time.

Cloud-based Delivery

Cloud-based delivery is any form of operation that a provider can offer through infrastructure, software and platforms. Therefore, if your business used Google Drive or Office 365, then you are making use of cloud-based delivery. In addition, other cloud-based delivery subscription-like Platform-as-a-Service(PaaS), Infrastructure-as-a-service(IaaS),etc, are made possible.

These are just a few of the different subscriptions as an individual or organization can purchase to use the software that is commonly referred to as Software-as-a-Service(SaaS), all thanks to technological innovations like virtualization and hypervisors.

You should know that Cloud-based delivery can dine both privately and publicly through the internet. It can be retained within an organizations network when delivered over an intranet. A combination of both is also possible.

Software as a Service(SaaS)

This cloud computing service is also referred to as cloud application services. This delivery model involves the provision of cloud computing services through authorized software or subscription.

The end-users don't need to purchase or install any hardware for this cloud-based delivery model in their respective location, and this is because in most case, SaaS applications operate directly via the web browser, this consequently eliminates the need to download or install the applications.

Below are some popular examples of SaaS:

- Google Apps
- Salesforce Dropbox
- Slack
- HubSpot
- Cisco WebEx

Platform as a Service(PaaS)

Platform as a service can also be referred to as cloud platform services. In a way, it possesses certain similarities with SaaS. However, the point of divergence is that PaaS offers a platform for the creation of software. On the other hand, SaaS enables access to software over the internet without the requirement of any platform.

The essence of PaaS as a cloud-based delivery model is to provide the end-users with the opportunity to create, operate, and also manage apps on the cloud computing architecture. In this delivery model, a third-party service provider organizes the hardware and software components.

Examples of PaaS are listed below:

- Windows Azure
- Force.com
- Magneto Commerce Cloud
- OpenShift

Infrastructure as a Service(IaaS)

It can also be referred to as Cloud Infrastructure Services. Here, this cloud-based delivery model supports computer hardware such as storage, data centre space, and networking technology as a service. It further helps to deliver virtualization technology and operating system—it is the responsibility of Infrastructure as a Service to manage middleware, application data and runtime environments.

Examples of Infrastructure as a Service includes:

- Amazon Web Services (AWS) EC2
- Google Compute Engine (GCE)
- Cisco Metapod

Having seen the components of google cloud architecture and how it functions and delivers services to the end-users we know look the essence of google cloud computing architecture;

Cost-Effectiveness

It is one of the most important reasons why you should make use of cloud computing architecture, and this is because cloud computing does not require any physical hardware investments. Consequently, this helps you to save significant capital costs.

Besides, there is no need to hire trained personnel for the maintenance of the hardware. Everything that deals with the purchasing and maintenance of your equipment is handled by the cloud service provider.

Access to the Latest Technology

Another essential reason why you need cloud computing architecture is to gain a competitive edge over your competitors. It enables you to get the most recent and modern tech applications whenever you need them. You would not have to spend any extra money or time on installation processes.

Fast Connectivity

With cloud computing, you are empowered to deploy your service in lesser chicks quickly. The consequent effect of quicker deployment is the ability for you to access the necessary resources for your system within fewer minutes.

Data Backup and Restoration

The moment the data is stored in a cloud storage architecture, it is easier to backup and recovers any lost dat without any hassles, this equally helps to save time that would have otherwise be spent on time taking process.

Reliability

It is one of the primary reasons why we use cloud computing services. One can rely on cloud computing architecture for an instant update about any modification or changes.

Remoteness

One can desire to work remotely from their home, and if you want to, cloud computing architecture is your primary precedence. It is because it allows employees who are working at remote locations to access all they need on cloud services easily. So far as there is internet connectivity, then, mobility is guaranteed.

Scalability and Flexibility

Cloud computing architecture is appropriate for businesses that have a growth or fluctuation bandwidth demand, and this is because it makes it very easy for businesses to scale up their cloud capacity by merely modifying their usage plan. If the business desires to scale down the cloud-based service provider can also make that possible. On the other hand, the degree of Flexibility that cloud computing architecture provides for businesses would give it a competitive edge over other competitors.

IT Readiness

Cloud computing architecture is known to influence brands to embrace the IT age more swiftly. It is quite vital since almost everyone uses smartphones. Therefore, by embracing the cloud, businesses are enabled to better communicate with their customers or even internal staffs on any platform at all, and this consequently results in an increased capacity to produce a more customized experience.

In all, it has become pronounced that architecture or cloud computing provides an abundant advantage for businesses. The adoption and implementation of Google cloud architecture give businesses a higher competitive edge in terms of increased productivity and lower cost.

Therefore, it is of importance for an ambitious organization that seek to succeed in the Post-IT age to leverage on the opportunities abundant in cloud computing architecture. So it is time to overlook the on-premise hosting and become very accessible through the most recent IT that are available on the cloud.

We have recent IT clouds like; Amazon web services, Google cloud platform, etc., whose infrastructure have been placed to meet peoples need or organization demands.

Google cloud platform let's organization take advantage of the powerful network and cloud computing architecture or the technologies that Google uses to deliver its products. Global companies like Coca-Cola and cutting edge technology stars like Spotify are already running sophisticated applications on the google cloud platform.

Putting all these together, we see how professional architecture as a course and its knowledge and application helps organizations in managing and providing cloud solutions infrastructure.

CHAPTER TWO - ARCHITECTING WITH GOOGLE COMPUTER ENGINE

In learning or getting ready to architect with the Google computer engine, a lot of things should be known and clearly understood.

Firstly, you should understand what a Google Computer Engine does in Google Cloud Architecture. The Google Computer Engine allows you to create and run virtual machines on Google Infrastructure. The computer engine offers a lot of things, including scale performance and value that would enable you to launch or start-up large computer clusters on Google's infrastructure. It has it also has its advantages that would allow you to run thousands of virtual CPU's on a system if the system has been originally designed to be fast and to give optimum consistency of performance, there are also no upfront investments. Google is preferably one of the best organizations as it is very efficient and plays out its role effectively. The Google Cloud Platform also supplies the Google Computer engine for infrastructure as in some service use cases like the IaaS. The Google Computer Engine also provides a very efficient computing infrastructure that allows us to select and consider the platform components that we will require. While working with the Google Computer Engine, we are required to administer, configure and carefully and expertly monitor the applications. It is our duty and responsibility to handle provision and manage the systems. At the same time, Google makes sure that the resources needed are available, reliable and ready for us to use them. One advantage attached to this is the fact that we now have absolute control of our systems, and we can also enjoy unlimited flexibility. The Google Computer Engine offers different kinds of machine types to suit your requirements and specifications configuration and also to meet your budget and needs, where you can also decide which operating systems, programming languages, frameworks, services, tech or development stacks you prefer.

The Google Cloud Platform is just Google's public cloud offering, and it can be compared to some web services like the Microsoft Azure and the Amazon web services. But unlike the other web services, the Google Cloud Platform is built and created upon the Google's vast and massive, cutting edge infrastructure that takes care of the traffic and workload of all the Google users.

Next, we have to get ourselves conversant with who a cloud architect is and what a cloud architect does and also the kind of skills he requires. A Cloud Architect is an IT professional whose work it is to oversee the cloud computing strategy for a company, and it includes a few things like the cloud adoption plans, cloud management and monitoring and the cloud application design. The cloud architect has to inspect and oversee the application architecture and the deployment in cloud environments, including the public cloud, the private cloud and the hybrid cloud. The cloud architects also have to stay informed and updated as they also act as consultants to their organizations on the latest trends, issues and information. Also, a Google Cloud architect must possess the following skills, or you must be able to do the following:

You must have the skill of programming languages: even while concentrating on the Google Cloud platform, knowing and understanding other programming languages like java, python, pearl etc. will improve and cover your bases for the cloud infrastructure and some cloud-native apps like the Kubernetes is also written in Go programming language.

Also, you must possess the multi-cloud architecture skill because the most convenient ways for organizations and enterprises to migrate their clouds most times if they follow the rules of privacy regulations is through the multi and hybrid strategies. In as much as it is advised to stick to one strategy on cloud suite, it is also detrimental as those who tend to have acquisitions can wind up with a multi-cloud strategy by default.

An almost normal and most essential skill a Cloud architect must-have is the Data storage skill, this includes the knowledge and information of infrastructure and hardware specifically for those who will be handling jobs with on-prem clouds, storage buckets, provisioning, capacity planning and of course data security. Also, you must possess content presentation and communication skills as they are essential and essential as it is known that cloud architects are often told to explain their work to their non-technical colleagues

Another skill to be possessed or acquired by a cloud architect is that of teamwork as cloud architects are often expected to lead a team. You should be able to manage people, handle ideas professionally and expertly and also solve problems.

Cloud architects must also learn how to change with the cloud, and the skill sets needed to work with it. They must be flexible to new technologies and must also have the attitude to pick them quickly and master them skillfully. So one that aspires to be a Google Cloud Architect and wants to begin or get started on building architectural diagrams of the Google Cloud Platform. You must learn, clear out and understand the following things which will help you fully understand how to develop or create a step by step diagram that runs and applies on the Google Cloud Platform we will be using a platform known as the Lucidchart.

Now we must understand the basics of the Lucidchart because this is one of the primary aspects of becoming a cloud architect. The Lucidchart is a web-based commercial or business service that allows users to join ideas, collaborate and work together in real-time to create flowcharts, UML designs, software prototypes, mind maps and organizational charts and many other diagram types. With the Lucidchart, you are allowed and free to share your dynamic ideas in the form of diagrams to the world. The Lucidchart is built on many web standards like the JavaScript and HTML5 and is also supported and allowed in many common web browsers like the Mozilla Firefox, the Google Chrome, Microsoft Edge, Safari and Internet Explorer. The Lucidchart platform has been recommended to users by Google as an ideal platform for building diagrams.

The Lucidchart has an online diagramming app that aids and assists real-time collaborative editing, it provides online diagramming to make it easy to draw and create flowcharts, org charts, wireframes UML, and more; it gives up many options for exporting and presenting your diagrams and is also equipped with well-stocked libraries of objects and templates too. This online diagramming app of the Lucidchart has its advantages and disadvantages. The benefits of the online diagramming app Lucidchart are it is very responsive, it is also easy to learn; it offers excellent collaboration and also provides the smooth user experience, the web app also works efficiently when offline and it also integrates with many other apps and services. It integrates with G Suite, Google Drive, Microsoft Office, Slack and more, and it imports Visio, OmniGirrafe to draw files, it runs on all major browsers. It is also stocked with shape libraries for many scenario's; like the flowcharts and process maps, AWS, Azure and GCP shapes, mockups and wireframes, UML, ER, and network diagrams, mind maps and Venn diagrams, org charts and BPMN diagrams. Then for its intuitive features, it has links and layers for interactive pictures, drag and drops functionality, auto prompt for quickly adding and connecting objects, interactive mockups with hotspots and current and future states, monitor processes, systems and goals through linking data and conditional formatting. It is also perfect for teams; like in the real-time collaboration, in editor group chat and comments, version control and revision history, build and share customized templates and make custom shape libraries. For the disadvantages, it doesn't allow desktop apps and also it is difficult to access its pricing and plan options.

Unlike some people who are not designers but require diagrams for some compelling presentations software like the flowchart and diagramming software will be needed for cases like that. The Lucidchart is just one of the best because it is a web app that works on any computer with a web browser and possesses an offline mode to keep you productive even when you are not connected to the internet. With this web app, it is easy to create and publish diagrams that look professional. One close competitor with the Lucidchart is the SmartDraw which is also an editors' choice. Still, it doesn't have a productive offline work mode like the Lucidchart but then it comes with a much bigger library and collection of objects and templates. The Lucidchart offers a few ranks of service. It provides a free personal account that can be used until infinity. Still, it provides limited storage and templates and only gives access to a library with basic shapes for creating diagrams and flowcharts. And if you wish to have access to more features and storage on this tier of the Lucidchart plan you'd have to pay for an upgrade as the in-app prices may be altered depending on the kind of selections you make during signup, it might be a monthly or an annual plan.

The Lucidchart has been improved, and its latest version has a few changes and upgrades. The newest version of the Lucidchart has integrations with the capacity and ability to take in or instead pull in and use data from elsewhere in your diagrams. Still, for this feature to be accessed, it must be paid for, you can now connect and get data imported from apps like Confluence, GitHub, JIRA, Slack, Salesforce and a lot of other apps. The main aim of these integrations is to make or create live diagrams that update in real-time and even possess more value beyond being illustrative.

How To Get Started With The Lucid Chart:

Firstly you need to signup, now the signup procedure is a simple one and doesn't require or disturb for a credit card. You can just easily put in your email address and create a password, or you can just sign up using Google or Office 365 account for validation, this is also the same with starting a new document, and it is straightforward whether you decide to use of the templates from the Lucidchart or you decide to make use of a blank document. For a blank document, you would know how to work your way around some shapes and text boxes because of its freehand, but if you decide to use a template, there are already a selection of squares, basic rectangles, text boxes and arrows on the page. If you check out the left bar, you'll notice that more shapes are made available. It is also straightforward to learn how to move the shapes around; duplicate them group them and ungroup them, rotate and resize them and a lot more. The user experience in the Lucidchart is more natural than in some other online diagramming apps, it is fast and responsive and figuring how to use it takes no stress or little brainpower when it comes to any diagramming app like the Lucidchart the selection of templates can either build or mar the diagramming app. When creating flowcharts, network infrastructure diagrams, floor plans and complicated designs templates and libraries are required as their absence in the diagramming work can and will leave a non-designer confused and unsure of what next to do or the next action to take. It is this aspect of diagramming that differentiates the diagramming software from the more general-purpose vector and graphics applications like for example the Adobe Illustrator. The primary selections of the Lucidchart are fully illustrated, most notably at the pro level. And this is because most of the very best software has an extensive and broad selection of shapes and templates for a crowd of uses. Even as good as the Lucidchart is and also as plentiful as its template and shapes selection is abundant, the SmartDraw's shapes and templates collection is much bigger and vast, and it also covers a lot of grounds that the Lucidchart doesn't cover at all. In the SmartDraw, you'll be able to find available templates and shapes for world maps, crime scenes, emergency evacuations and anatomy too. The Lucidchart doesn't possess all these templates because its selection isn't all that expansive and broad, so for diagrams that will require these listed specifications, the SmartDraw app should be used to work it out. Also, another necessary part of the diagramming software is how it aids to display your complete work or finished product. Using the Lucidchart diagrams can be exported to JPEG, PDF, SVG and PNG with transparent backgrounds and some others too. An option is also included on whether to export the CSV shape of your data.

Whether you work on a team of one or many, some times will present themselves, such times as when you need to share your work with others. It could be that you need to communicate an essential and complicated process to a client, or it could be that you want to collaborate on new project information from others. The Lucidchart proffers sharing solutions and options that make it less difficult to collaborate in real-time, process and gather feedback from others directly in the Lucidchart and also to change permission levels as the project evolves. And just because the Lucidchart is cloud-based and also available on all devices and browsers, there is certainly no barrier to working with others. Also, the Lucidchart is always up to date, and current on the latest developments or changes and nobody has to install expensive software on their computer or devices.

Now to understand the aspect of the collaboration tools in the Lucidchart, the Lucidchart has the capability and ability to collaborate with others at all account levels. We must also see that the Lucidchart was built for better collaboration from the origin or the beginning. However, there are still limitations of the account that still apply during the collaboration. A good instance is this one; when a person with a Team subscription invites a free account holder to collaborate on a diagram, now the file can only be edited by the free user if it has or possess fewer than 60 objects on it and also if it doesn't include any purposes that are limited to the paid accounts. A whole lot of diagramming apps aid and support collaboration, some of these diagramming apps is SmartDraw, Creately, and Visio. The competence of these apps to collaborate in real-time is soon becoming a standard feature in diagramming apps, most notably the cloud-based apps. On the invitation of another Lucidchart user or member to collaborate, you can make decisions of whether they can edit, edit and share, comment only or view only. In the Team and Enterprise accounts, the admins can include limits to the sharing permissions in such a way that it allows sharing only to other users within the organization. Collaboration performs much the same way as it usually does in Google Documents and some other G Suite apps, like Sheets and Slides. When more than one person has a file open, people can see who is in the document and the changes made as they work. Collaborators also have a chatbox for a live discussion of issues, and also a provision for commenting tools for asynchronous communication. Like I said earlier, the Lucidchart is very easy to learn and is adequately stocked with objects and templates and is an excellent choice for diagramming software. It provides exceptional and adequate collaboration support amongst team members. It is reasonably priced even though it also has some tremendous value-adding features, though it might be a little difficult selecting the plan that will work best for you and what you plan to do

CHAPTER THREE - PREPARATION FOR THE PROFESSIONAL CLOUD ARCHITECT EXAM

To ace this exam, you must prepare very well and study wide to acquire more information on the course. You must also acquire some skills to get more conversant with the questions that would be asked on the exam day. You must also learn to follow laid down rules as breaching of any of the rules will cost you some precious points in the exam.

Here are some tips and ideas on how you can prepare for the professional cloud architect exam and be confident about acing the test below:

1. **UNDERSTAND THE CONCEPTS OF THE HYBRID CLOUD.**

   To understand this subheading, you must first understand that a hybrid cloud is a combination of a private cloud joined with the use of public cloud services where one or more connection points exist between the environments. The main aim and objective are to combine services and data from a variety of cloud models to develop a unified automated and properly managed computing environment. The hybrid cloud services are compelling because it is known to combine the two cloud services to give businesses and firms more significant control over their private data. An example of the hybrid cloud is the AWS the Amazon Web Services with composition among the various platforms. It also enables convenient, on-demand network access to a shared source of configurable computing resources that can be quickly provisioned and released to the sources with little or no management effort or service provider interaction.

You must understand that there is a great deal of prominence on the connecting on-premises infrastructure to the Google Cloud Platform. You must clearly understand the picture and be able to make necessary connections on how to make the right chain. You must always understand completely the choices/ decisions and improvements that necessitate the corresponding loss of increasing in extent an enterprise data centre to the Google Cloud Platform.

Just like its other competitors, Google has a good number of channels to connect devices installed to be used only on the premises to the cloud. Every channel has its own specific and unique attribute that handles and takes care of a particular enterprise outline of an expected or supposed sequence of events. You must also be careful to understand the rules; the dos and don'ts of using one service against the other while trying to carry out the hybrid strategy. You must learn to mind and give attention to hybrid networking services offered by Google. The cloud VPN safely connects installed devices on the premises to the Google Cloud Platform VCP through the public internet. It is also cheap and safe, which slightly differs from the Cloud Interconnect, which delivers unmatched connectivity but is quite expensive. The direct peering is also a less expensive choice to the Cloud Interconnect that provides better performance than a VPN. It doesn't have an SLA, but it sure allows customers a direct connection to Google by a significant reduction on the fees.

2. KNOW HOW TO MOVE DATA TO GOOGLE CLOUD

Another essential and necessary step in migration is moving data to the Google cloud. A suitable technique is the online data transfer which is capable of moving large amounts of existing backup images and archived documents and files to extremely low cost and highly available storage provided through the Google's Nearline and Coldline storage classes. Google offers multiple services for moving data to Google Cloud Platform.

To carry out basic operations on the Google Cloud Storage, you must become conversant with the command-line tool. You must understand how to equally distance uploads, set up security and enhance the data migration with gsutil. The gsutil comes in handy to migrate a large number of files from local storage to the cloud.

The cloud storage transfer has become an ideal choice to move large amounts of data from other cloud platforms. The Transfer appliance is one of the best options when terabytes or petabytes of data need to be transferred to the Google Cloud Platform. It is also designed to reduce lengthy transfer times, making it faster, and it reduces risks that come with moving data over the internet to the public cloud. To use this Transfer appliance a customer requests for it from Google, and it is shipped into the customer's location. The customer's data is moved to the device and sent backed to Google, who now uploads it to the Google Cloud Storage service. After this process is done, the device is wiped by Google to ensure security measures and prevent underlying risks if the customer intends to migrate large datasets (a large file of related records on a computer medium) directly to the BigQuery Data Transfer Service, which automates data migration from SaaS applications to Google BigQuery on a planned, arranged and orderly basis.

To gain more understanding of this, we would research more into the usefulness of the BigQuery Data Transfer Service. The BigQuery Data Transfer Service is a Serverless, highly scalable, and cost-effective multi-cloud warehouse designed and programmed for business agility, speed and reliance. The BigQuery Data runs analytics at a scale of 26%-34% lower than three years TCO than cloud data warehouse alternatives, it aids to predict business outcomes and results with built-in machine learning and without the need to migrate data. It also aids customers to easily create comprehensive reports and dashboards using popular business intelligence tools, outside the normal and also assists to securely access and share analytical insights or ideas in your organization with a few clicks.

Here are some key features of the BigQuery

I) BigQuery Omni (private alpha)

It is a tractable, multi-cloud analytics solution, powered by Anthos that allows the user access to analyze data across clouds using standard SQL and BigQuery's familiar interface to answer questions and share results from your device across your datasets.

II) BigQuery ML

The BigQuery ML enables data scientists and data analysts to build and test out ML models on semi-structured data straight into the BigQuery, using simple SQL in a very small amount of time.

III) BigQuery BI Engine

The BigQuery BI Engine is an exceedingly fast-in-memory analysis service for BigQuery that allows customers and users to analyze or process large and complex datasets fairly with sub-second query response time and high concurrency. The Engine integrates with known tools which will help to accelerate data exploration and analysis.

3. LEARN GOOGLE CLOUD IAM IN DETAIL

The Google Cloud IAM (Identity and Access Management) allows administrators to give power to who can go to work on specific essential resources allowing the user maximum control and authority to manage Google Cloud resources centrally. The Google Cloud IAM gives up a central view into security policy across your entire enterprise for organizations and businesses with composite and complicated organizational structures and workgroups to reduce compliance processes. Due to the knowledge of the fact that a business's internal structure and policies can get composite fast and can also change dynamically, the Cloud IAM is specially designed to help simplify a lot of the complex changes. It is designed with a decent universal interface that lets the user manage access control across all Google Cloud resources consistently. Once this is known, it can be applied in any place.

Due to the inevitable fact that Permissions Control can be a time-consuming process, the program "Recommender" is written to aid admins in removing unwanted access to Google Cloud resources by the machine learning how to make smart access control recommendations. With this program, Recommender can easily detect or notice overly permissive access and put them in the correct order based on the same type of users in the enterprise and their access patterns. The Google Cloud IAM also makes the provision of tools to handle resource permissions with little or no complains and high automation. The users are granted access only to the specific tools needed to get their job done and completed, and the admins can easily grant permissions by default to an entire group of users. It also allows users to give access to cloud resources at the minimum level access well beyond the project level access. It creates more minute access control policies to resources based on attributes like IP address, resource type and more. These laid down policies ensure that accurate security controls are in a position when granting access to Google Cloud Resources. The Google Cloud IAM also lets you pay attention to business policies around your resources and makes carrying out instructions easy. It also has an in-built audit trail for the admins to get information on the history of permissions removal and delegation. Google Cloud also makes business and organizations identification easy. The Google Leverage Cloud Identity is an inbuilt managed identity created to harmonize the user's accounts over apps and projects efficiently. The Google Admin Console makes it very easy to set up single sign-on and configure two-factor authentication. You're also granted access to the Google Cloud Organization which allows and gives you the user to manage projects through the Resource Manager mainly.

Some features of the Google Cloud IAM are listed below:

I) No additional costs:

The Google Cloud IAM offers services for no extra or additional charges for all the cloud customers. You are only charged for the use of the other Google Cloud services. Both the access to the Google Cloud IAM is free of charge.

II) Supple Roles:

Previously before the Google Cloud IAMthe, only persons with access to users were the Owner, the editor and the viewer. So a large variety of services and resources now present additional Google Cloud IAM roles out of the box.

III) Single and simple access control interface:

The Google Cloud IAM gives up a non-complex and straightforward stable access control interface for all the Google Cloud services.

IV) An in-built audit trail

An in-built audit trail is made available and accessible to the admins to ease compliance procedures for your organization.

You must also understand the key differences between the user accounts and the service accounts. You must see that the real users use the user accounts while the service accounts are used by the system services such as databases, web servers, and mail transport agents. The service accounts are also a lot like the IAM (Identity and Access

Management) roles for EC2 where instances try to take over the meaning of a part. A service account is needed to connect the Compute engine VMs to the Google Cloud SQL instances. You must also see and understand how permissions propagate within the IAM hierarchy. You must also understand the four levels involved in setting IAM policies hierarchically; Organizational level, Folder level, Project level, Resource level.

The Organizational level:

The organization resource stands in for your company or enterprise. The IAM roles allowed at this level of the hierarchy are all gained or inherited by all resources under the organization.

The Folder level:

The folders can occupy or carry projects, other folders or even a combination of both. The roles allowed at the highest folder level will be obtained accordingly by other folders that are contained in the parent folder.

The Project level:

The projects stand-in for the trust limit or boundary among your company. Services among the same project have a default level of trust. Resources inherit identity and Access Management roles, given access at the project level within that particular project.

The Resource level:

Resources like Genomics data sets, Subtopics, and Compute Engine Instances aid in support of lower-level roles to enable you as a user permit certain other users to a single resource within a project just like the existing Cloud Storage and BigQuery ACL systems.

IAM policies are hierarchical and progress down the structure. The union of the policy is the active policy and the policy inherited from its parent.

You must also learn how to reflect your Google resource hierarchy structure into your organizational structure. It must reflect the structure of your company's organization or arrangement, whether it's a startup, SME, or a large corporation. An organization resource is advised for larger companies with more departments and teams where each team is in charge and control of their own set of applications and services. However, a startup might first play out with a flat resource hierarchy with no organization resource. You must also set policies at the project level organization level instead of the setting them at the resource level because as new resources are included, you might want them to inherit their policies from their parent resource automatically. Just like when new virtual machines are involved in the project through auto-scaling, they immediately and automatically inherit the policy on the project. You should also learn to use projects to group resources that share the same boundary. Just like resources for the same products can belong to or be owned by the same project. Also make sure to use labels to add metadata to a document, group, and filter resources.

You must always make sure to remember that the policies obtained by the child resources where gotten from the parent resources. And you must learn to grant roles at the minimum scope needed, just like when a user needs access to publish messages to a Pub/Subtopic he has to be granted the Publisher role to handle that topic. The Pub/Sub topics and subscriptions are resources that live under a project. If you would also like to limit project creation in your organization, the access organization policy must be changed to allow the Project Creator role to a group managed by you.

The Google Cloud Storage supports both the IAM and ACL policies. IAM is preferable when you want to protect buckets while the ACL's are great for safeguarding individual objects stored in buckets. You must understand their effective policies when they are both active.

4. SELECT THE APPROPRIATE CLOUD STORAGE AND DATABASE OFFERINGS

Unlike its competitors, the Google Cloud Platform has extraordinary and unique storage tiers that can deliver more value and services to the customers at a lower price, just the same way it is with the Google Cloud Platform database and broad data offerings.

There are a few things to consider when selecting the appropriate cloud storage:

I) You must consider the security capabilities as it is one of the most important factors restricting business holders from embracing the Cloud. Involving the use of a storage Cloud provider is more like handing over private information to a third party and a third eye with the hopes of safeguarding it. So in the process of selecting a Cloud Storage provider, one must ensure that all-sufficient security measures are taken. These include anti-virus software, data encryption, firewalls and routine security checkups.

II) You must also consider the data storage location; storing data in the Cloud involves storing it in an actual physical location, just transferred over the internet. When it comes to storing Cloud data you must understand your Cloud data location as storing data in a different country might attract a few issues, just like a change of laws in the country can affect who has access to the Cloud data. You should also consider the location if it is at risk for natural disasters like earthquakes, tsunamis, hurricanes and tornadoes. You should know your Cloud vendor plan in case of an emergency because it can play a significant role in protecting and saving your data.

III) Another thing to consider is the price. There are so many Cloud vendors striving for your business, so the prices have become very competitive. A lot of providers offer a particular amount of storage for free, but businesses that require a lot more storage will need to pay for their services. You should understand how the vendors charge their clients and work out the best pricing plan that is suitable for your company.

IV) The service level agreement should be a significant factor to be taken into consideration when deciding a cloud storage provider. The service level agreement primarily highlights the work of a vendor for your company and the responsibility of the client. The items included are about the kind of data to be stored, how it will be stored and protected, how the problems will be solved and a lot more. Make sure you understand the prospective cloud vendor's service level agreement entails.

V) The last but not the least thing to consider is tech support, and this is because problems will always arise at different occasions. But you must also understand that the cloud provider can be contacted for assistance, so while you choose a vendor to ensure to ask them how they handle each support, you should also find out from them their available days and note how quickly they respond to problems. You must observe all these essential factors in a vendor to avoid the ones who do not meet up with your required needs.

Also, you must take note of when to use regional, multi-regional, nearline and coldline storage tiers when uploading and storing data in object storage. A nearline is used for when data is accessed at least once a month, and the coldline makes sense when the information is accessed only once a year.

The architects will be required to choose among a lot of different databases depending on their uses. You must also get used to the core and most essential aspects of the database, Cloud SQL, Cloud Spanner, Cloud Big table and BigQuery. The Cloud SQL gives up compatibility with already present MySQL and PostgreSQL databases. The BigQuery is meant for the storage and retrieving of large datasets with aid and support for ANSI SQL. And no, it is not a replacement to a NoSQL and RDBMS database server. The Cloud Dataflow is useful when data pipelines are to be built for streaming and batch processing scenarios.

CHAPTER FOUR - GETTING STARTED WITH GOOGLE KUBERNETES ENGINE

Kubernetes is an open-source container platform that removes so many of the manual processes involved in unfolding, scaling and managing containerized applications.

Google originally designed Kubernetes, and it is maintained by the Cloud Native Computing Foundation currently. Kubernetes aims to provide a "platform for automating deployment, scaling, and operations of application containers across clusters of hosts". It works with a range of container tools, including Docker.

So many cloud services offer a Kubernetes-based platform or infrastructure as a service (PaaS or IaaS) on which Kubernetes can be deployed as a platform-providing service. Many companies also provide their own branded Kubernetes distributions.

Created by the same developers that built Kubernetes, Google Kubernetes Engine (GKE) is an easy to use cloud-based Kubernetes service for running containerized applications. GKE can help you implement a successful

Kubernetes strategy for your applications in the cloud. With Anthos, Google offers a consistent Kubernetes experience for your applications across on-premises and multiple clouds. Using Anthos, you get a reliable, efficient, and trusted way to run Kubernetes clusters, anywhere.

Brief History About Kubernetes

he Greek word for Kubernetes is`κυβερνήτης`, meaning "helmsman" or "pilot." and the Tetymological root of cybernetics was founded by Joe Beda, Brendan Burns, and Craig McLuckie, who was quickly joined by other Google engineers including Brian Grant and Tim Hockin, and was first announced by Google in mid-2014. Google's Borg system heavily influences its development and design, and many of the top contributors to the project previously worked on Borg. The original codename for Kubernetes within Google was Project 7, a reference to the Star Trek ex-Borg character Seven of Nine. The seven spokes on the wheel of the Kubernetes logo are a reference to that codename. The original Borg project was written entirely in C++[10], but the rewritten Kubernetes system is implemented in Go.

Kubernetes v1.0 was released on July 21, 2015. Alongside with the Kubernetes v1.0 release, Google partnered with the Linux Foundation to form the Cloud Native Computing Foundation (CNCF) and offered Kubernetes as a seed technology. On March 6, 2018, Kubernetes Project reached ninth place in commits at GitHub and second place in authors and issues to the Linux kernel.

Features Of Kubernetes Google Engine

KUBERNETE PODS

A pod can be defined as a higher level of abstraction grouping containerized components. A pod consists of more than one containers that are guaranteed to be co-located on the host machine and can share resources. The basic scheduling unit in Kubernetes is a pod.

Each pod in Kubernetes is assigned a unique Pod IP address within the cluster, which allows applications to use ports without the risk of conflict. Within the pod, all containers can reference each other on localhost, but a container within one pod has no way of directly addressing another container within another pod; for that, it has to use the Pod IP Address. An application developer should never try to use the Pod IP Address though, to reference/invoke a capability in another pod, as Pod IP addresses are temporary - the specific pod that they are referencing may be assigned to another Pod IP address on restart. Instead, they should use a reference to a Service, which holds a reference to the target pod at the specific Pod IP Address.

A pod can define a volume, such as a local disk directory or a network disk, and expose it to the containers in the pod. Pods can be managed manually through the Kubernetes API, or their management can be delegated to a controller. Such volumes are also the basis for the Kubernetes features of Configure Maps (to provide access to configuration through the filesystem visible to the container) and Secrets (to provide access to credentials needed to access remote resources securely, by delivering those credentials on the filesystem visible only to authorized containers).

CLUSTERORCHESTRATIONWITH GKE

The Kubernetes open-source cluster management system powers GKE clusters. Kubernetes provides the mechanisms through which you interact with your cluster. You use Kubernetes commands and resources to deploy and manage your applications, perform administration tasks, set policies, and monitor the health of your deployed workloads.

Kubernetes draws on the same design principles that run popular Google services and provides the same benefits: automatic management, monitoring and liveness probes for application containers, automatic scaling, rolling updates, and more. When you run your applications on a cluster, you're using technology based on Google's 10+ years of experience running production workloads in containers.

KUBERNETES ON GOOGLE CLOUD

When you run a GKE cluster, you also gain the benefit of advanced cluster management features that Google Cloud provides. These include:

- Google Cloud's load-balancing for Compute Engine instances
- Node pools to designate subsets of nodes within a cluster for additional flexibility

- Automatic scaling of your cluster's node instance count
- Automatic upgrades for your cluster's node software
- Node auto-repair to maintain node health and availability
- Logging and monitoring with Google Cloud's operations suite for visibility into your cluster.

ReplicaSets

A ReplicaSet's purpose is to maintain a stable set of replica Pods running at any given time. As such, it is often used to guarantee the availability of a specified number of identical Pods.

The ReplicaSets can also be said to be a grouping mechanism that lets Kubernetes maintain the number of instances that have been declared for a given pod. The definition of a Replica Set uses a selector, whose evaluation will result in identifying all pods that are associated with it.

Services

Simplified view showing how Services interact with Pod networking in a Kubernetes cluster

A Kubernetes service is a set of pods that work together, such as one tier of a multi-tier application. A label selector defines the set of pods that constitute a service. Kubernetes provides two modes of service discovery, using environmental variables or using Kubernetes DNS. Service discovery assigns a stable IP address and DNS name to the service, and load balances traffic in a round-robin manner to network connections of that IP address among the pods matching the selector (even as failures cause the pods to move from machine to machine). By default, service is exposed inside a cluster (e.g., back end pods might be grouped into service, with requests from the front-end pods load-balanced among them), but service can also be exposed outside a cluster (e.g., for clients to reach front-end pods).

Volumes

Filesystems in the Kubernetes container provide temporary storage; by default, this means that a restart of the pod will wipe out any data on such containers. Therefore, this form of storage is quite limiting in anything but trivial applications. A Kubernetes Volume provides persistent storage that exists for the lifetime of the pod itself. This storage can also be used as shared disk space for containers within the pod. Volumes are mounted at specific mount points within the container, which are defined by the pod configuration, and cannot mount onto other sizes or link to other formats. The same size can be installed at different points in the filesystem tree by different containers.

Namespaces

Kubernetes provides a partitioning of the resources it manages into non-overlapping sets called namespaces. They are intended for use in environments with many users spread across multiple teams, or projects, or even separating environments like development, test, and production.

Configuration Maps and Secrets

A common application challenge is deciding where to store and manage configuration information, some of which may contain sensitive data. Configuration data can be anything as fine-grained as individual properties or coarse-grained information like entire configuration files or JSON / XML documents. Kubernetes provides two closely related mechanisms to deal with this need: "configmaps" and "secrets", both of which allow for configuration changes to be made without requiring an application build. The data from configuration maps and secrets will be made available to every single instance of the application to which these objects have been bound via the deployment. A secret or a configuration map is only sent to a node if a pod on that node requires it. Kubernetes will keep it in memory on that node. Once the pod that depends on the secret or configmap is deleted, the in-memory copy of all bound secrets and configuration maps are removed as well. The data is accessible to the pod through one of two ways: a) as environment variables (which will be created by Kubernetes when the pod is started) or b) available on the container filesystem that is visible only from within the pod.

The data itself is stored on the master, which is a highly secured machine which nobody should have login access to, the most significant difference between a secret and a configuration map is that the content of the data in secret is base64 encoded. (On newer k8s versions, secrets are stored encrypted in etc.)

StatefulSets

It is straightforward to address the scaling of stateless applications: one simply adds more running pods—which is something that Kubernetes does very well. Stateful workloads are much harder because the state needs to be preserved if a pod is restarted, and if the application is scaled up or down, then the state may need to be redistributed. Databases are an example of stateful workloads. When run in high-availability mode, many databases come with the notion of a primary instance and a secondary situation (s). In this case, the idea of the ordering of cases is essential. Other applications like Kafka distribute the data amongst their brokers—so one broker is not the same as another. In this case, the notion of instance, uniqueness is essential. StatefulSets[30] are controllers (see Controller Manager, below) that are provided by Kubernetes that enforce the properties of uniqueness and ordering amongst instances of a pod and can be used to run stateful applications.

DaemonSets

Usually, the location where pods are run is determined by the algorithm implemented in the Kubernetes Scheduler. For some use cases, though, there could be a need to run a pod on every single node in the cluster. It is useful for use cases like log collection, ingress controllers, and storage services. The ability to do this kind of pod scheduling is implemented by the feature called DaemonSets.

Secrets

Secrets contain the keys, passwords and OAuth tokens for the pod.

Managing Kubernetes objects

Kubernetes provides some mechanisms that allow one to manage, select, or manipulate its objects.

Labels and selectors

Kubernetes enables clients (users or internal components) to attach keys called "labels" to any API object in the system, such as pods and nodes. Correspondingly, "label selectors" are queries against labels that resolve to match objects. When a service is defined, one can define the label selectors that will be used by the service router/load balancer to select the pod instances that the traffic will be routed to, thus, simply changing the labels of the pods or changing the label selectors on the service can be used to control which pods get traffic and which don't, which can be used to support various deployment patterns like blue-green deployments or A-B testing. This capability to dynamically control how services utilize implementing resources provides a loose coupling within the infrastructure. All signs are pointing to Kubernetes becoming the defacto standard for container orchestration platforms. Let's say you've done your research, and you know you want to use Kubernetes as your content management system. All well and good. You also know you have two main cloud hosting options: Amazon Web Services (AWS) and Google Cloud Platform (GCP).

Amazon's obvious choice, as many developers have limited exposure to and experience with GCP and Google Container Engine (GKE).

However, if you want to run Kubernetes on AWS, you have a lot of work ahead of you. If you're looking for container-based workflows, GCP will make Kubernetes a lot easier to manage and keep up to date. Since Google created Kubernetes, GKE gives you a Kubernetes cluster out of the box. In other words, rather than setting up Kubernetes on AWS, there's a better option: letting the people who built Kubernetes also host it.

The Benefits Of Running Kubernetes On Google Container Engine

Kubernetes on GKE vs. AWS

Let's start with the premise that it's better to run Kubernetes on GCP than on AWS. A reasonable question to ask is why - what's the difference?

The most straightforward answer is that Google has a hand in developing Kubernetes, so Google supports new Kubernetes features automatically and faster - sometimes much, much faster than other cloud providers. Google Container Engine (GKE) supports the latest and most excellent versions of Kubernetes sooner than other cloud providers.

If you know you want to use Kubernetes, then you'll probably spend less time and money setting it up on Google than on AWS. Let's look at what this means in real terms.

Closed vs. Open Source

Amazon EC2 Container Service (ECS) is Amazon's attempt to build a container cluster. It's entirely closed source, whereas Kubernetes is entirely open source. You can see who's developing Kubernetes (and what they're developing), and you're not locked into a cloud provider (AWS or Google).

Uncommon vs. Familiar Paradigms

Amazon has home-baked their container cluster software, and the skills you'll need to build when using ECS are different than those used on other platforms. ECS is a hodgepodge of Amazon's other services glued together, meaning it's neither robust nor architected in a way that makes it easy to use on production workloads.

The skills you develop with Kubernetes can be applied to several other products and systems, whereas the skills you build using ECS is very specialized and not applicable to most of the other work you do. As a result, running either ECS or Kubernetes on AWS will require a lot of manual effort, and you'll need to jump through quite a few hoops.

Automation vs. Manual Effort

Along those lines, if you want to use Kubernetes, GKE shortens the learning curve considerably because Google sets up its baseline functionality for you. With GKE, you can turn on a Kubernetes cluster and be up and running in 10 minutes, whereas on AWS you have to do a lot of work to understand how to set up the cluster, what tooling to use and how to build the new cluster when you're ready. You'll also have to troubleshoot any issues that arise and then be able to assess if the cluster is up and running the way you expected.

GKE eliminates these time-consuming steps. Just tell GKE some basic things about your cluster, and it will automagically bootstrap your cluster for you. GKE saves a ton of headache and time in the actual creation of the cluster, and you can start deploying applications on the cluster quickly without the overhead of having to keep the cluster running in the first place.

Simple vs. Complex Integration

AWS doesn't have a managed Kubernetes installation as GKE does. GKE, on the other hand, has Google backing and integrates with all of Google's other tooling. It comes with built-in logging, log management and monitoring at both the host and container levels. Unlike AWS, it can give you automatic autoscaling, automatic hardware management and automatic version updates. It generally gives you a production-ready cluster with a more batteries-included approach than if you were building everything by hand on AWS.

The AWS/GCP Decision Is Yours

Community support for containerization clusters is solidifying around Kubernetes. Because Kubernetes and GKE both developed internally within Google, Google engineers are paid to support all Kubernetes features sooner (and better) than other cloud services. Amazon isn't paying their engineers to make Kubernetes run better on Amazon.

With GKE, you get a production-ready Kubernetes cluster with all the necessary tooling, along with ongoing support needed to make sure your packages and versions stay current. GKE takes care of security defaults for you and integrates with other Google services. This combination requires less overhead in managing the cluster and makes it more seamless to use in the long run.

To be clear, Fairwinds can handle Kubernetes on AWS and GCP. Either solution works just fine for us. However, if you have the political capital and ability to choose (if, for example, you're not already an Amazon shop), GKE will make your life easier.

Simply put, Kubernetes is better on GKE than on AWS. Running Kubernetes on GCP will save you time and money, as well as give you a shorter learning curve, more synergies and an all-around better experience.

Advantages Of Kubernetes

1. Using Kubernetes and its vast ecosystem can improve your productivity

If Kubernetes is appropriately implemented into your engineering workflows, it can lead to significant productivity gains. Especially the vast Kubernetes ecosystem, which can best be shown with the CNCF Landscape, helps to use Kubernetes easily and efficiently reducing the negative impact of its general complexity. By relying on some existing tools specifically made for cloud-native software, you can get solutions that you could hardly ever build yourself.

As an example: Our company recently added the open-source development tool DevSpace to CNCF, which lets you set up and standardize the deployment and testing workflow for every developer on your team. Other tools such as Drone let you quickly create CI/CD pipelines for Kubernetes and tools like Prometheus make monitoring more straightforward than ever. This plethora of tools available in the ecosystem shorten release cycles drastically, professionalizes engineering workflows and eventually improves the software quality from development to production. Of course, this huge selection of technologies also helps you to customize everything exactly to your needs. As an additional bonus, most of the tools in the k8s ecosystem are open-source and thus free to use.

2. Kubernetes and a cloud-native tech stack attracts talent

Many software engineers want to work in companies that use modern and exciting technologies. Kubernetes is definitively one of them being ranked as the 3rd most wanted platforms in the Stack Overflow Developer Survey 2019. Combined with an efficient workflow with other cloud-native tools, your technology stack and processes will be very attractive for potential applicants. Also for your current workforce, it can be very motivating to work with something new, which improves the general satisfaction in your dev teams and can even reduce employee turnover in the long run. This advantage of Kubernetes is often overlooked, but given the shortage of tech talent, it can be a material benefit for your organization.

3. Kubernetes is a future proof solution

If you decide to use Kubernetes, you can be pretty sure that this solution is feasible for many years for several reasons:

All major cloud vendors are supporting Kubernetes providing out-of-the-box solutions for it.

Alternative container orchestration solutions are far behind k8s in terms of adoption, support by cloud vendors and their ecosystems. Even companies previously focused on competing technologies are now endorsing Kubernetes: Docker is offering Docker Kubernetes Service instead of just Docker Swarm solutions, and Mesosphere changed its name to D2IQ to be more open for Kubernetes and not purely focused on Apache Mesos.

And of course: The Kubernetes ecosystem is growing incredibly fast, and new products supporting different needs on top of the Kubernetes platform are being released every day.

Kubernetes is also future proof from an individual perspective: If you expect your user base to grow even to a huge audience, you can be sure that Kubernetes can handle it because it is designed to support large, distributed systems and it was originally developed by Google engineers and backed by their experience in building scalable platforms like Borg. The same goes for your application if it grows and becomes more complex. Here, microservice architectures often come into play, and for these, Kubernetes is the technology of choice as of today. And finally, if you want to switch your cloud vendor for some reason, e.g. moving from Amazon Web Services (AWS) to Microsoft Azure, you can easily find a very similar Kubernetes service from a different provider and Kubernetes itself makes such a switch relatively seamless preventing you from vendor lock-in.

4. Kubernetes helps to make your application run more stable

If you need to be sure that your application is up and running very reliably, Kubernetes can support you in this. For example, it allows you to have rolling updates to change your software without downtime. It is further possible to set up Kubernetes in a way that it supports high availability applications. If you are using the public cloud services of major vendors, you can be pretty sure to reach a very high uptime. (However, this is of course also possible with other technologies and infrastructures but often involves considerably more effort.)

5. Kubernetes can be cheaper than its alternatives

Another advantage of k8s is that it can sometimes be cheaper than other solutions (depending on your application). Since the platform itself has some general computing needs, it is usually more expensive for very small applications. However, the larger your computing resource needs, the less important are these basic infrastructure needs for the overall cost calculation. In such cases, other factors become more important. For example, Kubernetes can auto-scale depending on the needs of your application and the incoming traffic and load processed by your applications. That means that Kubernetes can scale up your applications and its required resources during peak times but also scale down your infrastructure during less busy times of the year, week or even hours of the day. That means you pay less if there is not much going on. Overall, this leads to high utilization and prevents you from paying for resources that you do not need.

The relatively new concept of "nodeless Kubernetes" with solutions such as Virtual Kubelet or elot provides additional potential for saving infrastructure cost.

Overall, Kubernetes can thus be cheaper in some cases and more expensive in others, and there is always potential to reduce the cost of running it. For this, you need to evaluate it for your specific application and compare the different providers for your needs (however, for the choice of your cloud provider, more factors than just cost will usually play a role).

Disadvantages Of Kubernetes

1. Kubernetes can be an overkill for simple applications

Kubernetes is a complex but powerful technology that allows you to run the software in a cloud environment at a massive scale pretty efficiently. However, if you do not intend to develop anything complex for a large or distributed audience (so, you are not building a worldwide online shop with thousands of customers for example) or with high computing resource needs (e.g. machine learning applications), there is not much benefit for you from the technical power of k8s. Let's say you just want to develop a website showing the opening hours and location of your business. Then you should not use Kubernetes because this is not what it was made for; however, one cannot generally say that every machine learning software should run with Kubernetes and no simple website should. It is just way more likely that it will be beneficial in the first case than in the other one.

2. Kubernetes is very complex and can reduce productivity

Kubernetes is infamously known for its complexity. Especially for developers not familiar with infrastructure technologies, it can be very hard to work with; however, if you want to practice the DevOps approach, developers need to get access to and deploy to Kubernetes as early as possible during the development lifecycle, so they can test their code quickly and early on to prevent costly mistakes later on in production. Even though there is a clear tendency to make Kubernetes easier and more accessible (DevSpace is, for example, striving to be the most comfortable and fastest Kubernetes tool for developers), it is still advisable to have at least one Kubernetes expert with a profound understanding of k8s on every engineering team. Someone with this skill can either be hired, which is still relatively expensive - the average salary in the US for people with k8s skills is more than $140,000, or be trained, which will take a while.

In any case, your development team will have to adapt some of its processes to become genuinely cloud-native. At least in the short term, this may result in reduced productivity and longer release cycles. (However, k8s can also boost your productivity in the long run, if done right)

3. The transition to Kubernetes can be cumbersome

Since most companies cannot start on a green field, your existing software needs to be adapted to run smoothly with Kubernetes or at least alongside the newly built application that will run on Kubernetes. It is hard to estimate how much effort this requires as this depends heavily on the software (e.g. is it already containerized, which programming language is used). Additionally, some processes need to be adapted to the new environment, especially deployment processes. Even with experienced staff on-site, the adoption of Kubernetes might still be a challenge and requires quite some effort and time.

4. Kubernetes can be more expensive than its alternatives

I have already described that Kubernetes can be cheaper than using alternative technologies. However, it can also be more expensive, and this is because all of the previously mentioned disadvantages cost time of your engineers that is not spent on creating new "tangible" business value.

If your engineers are spending their time getting an existing, running application to run in Kubernetes, their goal is to reach the status quo with different technology.

And if they reach this goal, the users of this application will not immediately see any benefits of this migration (however, there might be some subtle advantages, such as improved stability). Since engineering time is a highly valuable resource, this should be considered for your decision to adopt Kubernetes.

Besides this indirect cost, sometimes the infrastructure cost of running Kubernetes is simply higher than for alternative infrastructures, especially for small applications as Kubernetes itself has some computing needs. Again, taking the simplified example of a simple website, it might just be cheaper to choose a much simpler infrastructure, such as a single VM or hosting platforms such as Heroku or Netlify.

Conclusion

There is no easy answer if adopting Kubernetes is the right choice for you or not. It depends on your specific needs and priorities, and many technical reasons were not even mentioned here. If you are starting with a new project, if you work in a startup that intends to scale and wants to develop more than just a quick MVP or if you need to upgrade a legacy application, Kubernetes might be a good choice giving you a lot of flexibility, power and scalability. However, it always requires an investment of time because new skills have to be acquired and new workflows have to be established in your dev team.

If done right, however, investing the time to learn and adopt Kubernetes will often pay off in the future due to better service quality, a higher productivity level and a more motivated workforce.

In any case, you should make an informed decision, and there are many good reasons to go for Kubernetes or leave it. I hope this post will help you in getting closer to making the right decision for you.

CHAPTER FIVE- DESIGNING AND PLANNING A CLOUD SOLUTION ARCHITECTURE

There is quite a problem most cloud projects face that may cause them to fail and crash, and this happens as a result of wrong or missing architecture and design methods.

Usually, lack of a general understanding of methods that need to be applied to prepare suitable cloud computing solutions could lead the project to a rough end with developed problems like:

- Lack of governance and weak or no securities at all.
- Saturation of resources
- Inefficient utilization of resources
- Lack of scalability
- Lack of elasticity

A very solid cloud architecture design is reliable, and it forms a backbone of your cloud, and this begins with smart decisions made by you. A suitable and secure method of architecture design is required for taking advantage of the inherent strengths of cloud computing. Presently, cloud computing is quite different from what it was in the past [some years ago], and it will develop in a few years to come and more. Building or designing an effective cloud strategy today might save you the risks from tomorrow.

So, what are the emerging best methods and practices? What are the proper ways to leverage cloud computing systems? What are the proper techniques to build cloud computing systems? What are the appropriate ways to design cloud computing systems?

Well, just like many other IT architecture, there is no single solution. True, there are different situations and needs. Still, a good understanding of methods will save you from failing and pitfalls and will also help you evaluate your needs like Infrastructure, scalability, applications, security and compliance and as well build the proper cloud architecture. The best practices these days are around "fast planning".

Designing a Good Cloud Architecture

The following are common and best steps and practices you can employ to design your cloud architecture:

1. Multi-Cloud method: According to IDC Predictions of Worldwide Cloud in 2017, about 85% of Enterprise IT businesses in 2018 have committed to multi-cloud architectures; this commitment helped them to increase the rate and provided huge opportunities to secure massive growth in their business field. Today, businesses need to seek help from one or multiple cloud-based service provider to provide security for

their business data and other relevant information. Changing from one cloud to another could be possible if you make use of an excellent multi-cloud strategy. A good multi-cloud strategy will also ensure that you run the services balanced between two or more clouds. No one size automatically fits in all, through planning a multi-cloud method, you will comfortably perform tasks using the best performance ratio.

While engaging in the multi-cloud method, the following should be considered:

- A service you might be getting with a cloud provider might be performing better on the other. Critically check how services respond then create the right mixture for your business across multiple clouds.
- It is always a good thing to employ open-source replacements for any native service that you could replace. At start-up [in a short run], getting into a trap of native service will be easy but after experiencing expansion and growth in the long term, getting into such trap becomes difficult. When you use open-source replacements from the start, you experience suppleness with different services without being held and stuck with native services.

2. Optimize your cost: Cloud cost optimization strategy is a very comfortable and trusted way to reduce your overall cloud spends and reduce your cost to a

minimum. With this strategy, you can spot and identify mismanaged resources, eliminating waste, and you can right-size computing services. The following steps will guide you in optimizing your cloud cost, and it is required you keep them in mind:

- Have a defined baseline: Your starting point should be well defined and understood; something that will give you an awareness of situations. You can preferably use a tool like the free AWS Cost Explorer; this will help you to quickly gain an understanding of cloud spending at both macro and micro levels. Having a defined baseline will enable you to measure the impact of your optimization efforts over time.
- Right-Size your instances: According to Flexera 2020 State of the Cloud Report, A lot of organizations right-size their cases. Right-sizing your case is a primary way of controlling cloud costs.

  Spot instances, Reserve instances and Saving plans are three best right-sizing tactics.

  Spot instances are less expensive, and it offers the greatest savings. Here, the cloud provider does not commit to providing the case at a specified time. You can comfortably choose what you would like to run and the duration as well. Spot instances are ideal and recommended for flexible workloads like batch processing.

For Reserve instances and saving plans, they offer similar sized savings at up to 72% or so. Regardless of their differences, their similarity is a steep discount in exchange for a single or multi-year commitment to the platform.

As workloads change, instance needs will change too. Therefore, for instance, right-sizing should be an ongoing exercise and not just a single or once approach.

- Another way you can reduce cost in selecting the right types, configurations and storage solutions to suit your needs. There is no extra cost in implementing auto-scaling to be able to scale when required horizontally or to scale down when necessary.
- Reduce the cost of data transfer: One of the things you should know is that Data transfer is free in the same region. Therefore, you should ensure that your Object storage and Computer Services are in the same area. For example, to download the file a file from another AWS region, AWS will charge $0.02/GB.

  It may be cheaper to replicate your Object Storage bucket to a different region using a feature built into S3 called cross-region replication. It will enable you to get better performance along with cost-benefit.

  Let me expand your understanding using the AWS S3's example. Take, for instance, 1GB data in location"B" is anticipated to be transferred 20 times to EC2 in location "A". If you initiate inter-region transfer, you will pay about $0.20 for data transfer [20 * 0.02]. However, if you first download it to mirror S3 bucket in location "A", then you will just have to pay $0.02 for transfer and also pay $0.03 for storage over a month, and it is 75% cheaper.

- Compress Data Before Storage: Compressing data reduces your storage requirements and subsequently reduces the cost of storage. A comfortable and less stressful way is to use a fast compression algorithm. A preferable algorithm to use is LZ4; it is a lossless compression algorithm which provides compression speed at 400 MB/s per core [0.16 Bytes/cycle]. It also features a high-speed decoder, with speed in, multiple GB/s per core [0.71 Bytes/cycle].

3. Operational Excellence: One thing that drives excellence is an effective operation. To achieve this, you should be able to manage workloads. These are procedures and practices you should follow to manage workloads:

   - Align processes - Operations should be automated with codes.
   - Collect metrics from various resources and then align processes on the business needs.
   - Make Incremental Changes - To avoid failure in cases of unexpected events and to identify and

get rid of the cause, you should make small incremental changes instead of making changes in big packages.

- Unexpected events - For sure, unforeseen circumstances may arise; always test for unforeseen circumstances. Capture events and failures too and then design a room for improvements.
- Maintain documentation - Always keep your procedures and documentation up to date and avoid any form of delay, which may be useful for understanding and troubleshooting purposes.

4. Performance/Efficiency: A lot of performance benefits could be achieved if you design your environment with the right platform and in the right way. But the question is, how efficiently you can manage your computer resources to meet your requirements?

   These are four steps that you can follow to manage to compute resources:

   - Make use of Latest Technologies -Your applications and services should be built on an evolved platform. High performances environment and templates can give you an advantage of a better performing cloud.
   - Right-sized - You should choose the right services and observe your environment, studying what services are best suitable to match what you demand.

- Put automation in place. When you implement automation and put automation in place, you get the ability to experiment more often and minimize manual processes.
- Listen to your application -based on your evolving requirements, a cloud service you chose yesterday might not be the best today. Identify and know your applications resource requirements such as RAM, CPU, Storage, etc.

5. Reliability: Before architecting your cloud, you should ensure to take on the best practices. Your starting should be reliable. Your system should have the ability to recover from the outage and be able to meet demands dynamically. Your system should effectively and technically work in every scenario. Ensure you follow the following practices:
    - You should critically think of how you can recover from failure quickly. A proper approach to this is to design an automated recovery process and as well as anticipate failures. You should be aware of how failures would happen and how well you can respond to failures when they come up.
    - Do not share a common point of failure and set up a redundant architecture to avoid downtime. Design a highly available architecture.
    - Stick to processes and follow them. You should always create a process to make any changes in

monolithic architecture, covering changes in demand, monitoring resources and executing.

- Stop guessing capacity - The idea of guessing can either produce under-provision or over-provision. Guessing will lead you to either have an outage, or your systems may be left sitting idle.
- Make use of a redundant network. This will have you eliminate network failures.

6. Proactive Planning: Just like the famous saying goes "prevention is better than cure", always have a theory that your hardware will fail and follow such theory. Have a mechanism to deal with unknown failures and catastrophes before it affects you.

   You should be able to consider the following practices:

   - Don't predict your capacity - Avoid guessing and predicting your capacity. A wrong prediction might lead you to expensive resources, or you might have to deal with performance implications of limited size.
   - Automate - You can create and replicate systems with automation; this will make your architecture dynamic. Automation reduces the risk of design changes.
   - Be data-driven - Your data will inform you of the choice you have to make. In the cloud, you can

collect data on the behaviour of your application needs and identify what's best.

- Design Evolutionary Architecture - An evolutionary architecture enable changes in architecture over time. Rapid changes in a business environment could hinder the decisions to deliver, but following best practices and implementing them while designing cloud architecture can help you evolve.

7. Security: Securing your cloud environment should be your primary concern, especially when you are running your apps on a cloud or when you are migrating to another cloud. Cloud security is just everything! You don't just think security at critical levels and in time of failing. Your safety should be hardened at all layers. Your Cloud and data could be affected by unauthorized actions and operations when it's not secured and protected. That is why you must discover and harden your securities layers. Some ways to learn and ensure protection for your cloud environment are:

   - Protect your Data - Closely observe and focus on your data protection.

     * Data should be classified in different segments. For example, the Public segment, the private segment, shared, etc.

     * Hide your data. You can achieve this by creating code or something private. Your data should be well encrypted.

* Create different policies to prevent Accidental and unplanned overwrites and changes.

- • Take a detailed assessment of your infrastructure from policies to patches ensuring your infrastructure is secured and protected. These are good and better practices to this approach:
  * Use antivirus and firewalls to protect your infrastructure and harden your security with all individual OS patches regularly.
  * Periodic checks and Traceability - Always take on periodic checks and identify loop-holes. Check the ports, the layers and trace on how someone can hack into an environment.
- • Follow Access Specifiers - In as much as you are responsible for securing your data, OS and application, it is always advisable that you do not use admin or root logins unless they are required. Even if it is necessary, you must do the following:
  * Create password logging policies for yourself.
  * Use keys Management services
  * Enable multi-factor authentication
  * *You should also limit access to your data or your apps from other apps or 3rd party tools.
  * Assign least privilege access system

8. Automate Security: Cloud enables automation of several events which improves both your system's stability and the efficiency of your organization. You should have an awareness of everything and be responsible for all the security events such as 2FA, SSH, encryption, authenticity etc. One of the safest things to do while moving fast is to test and audit your environment. You can implement continuous monitoring and automation of controls to minimize exposure to security risks.

   Your security should be automated at all events. To do this, you can set notifications or set emails whenever someone accesses the cloud.

9. Caching: This is one approach that can boost your application performance and cost-efficiency of an application. Caching is a simple method or technique of storing in your memory, data and information that are used frequently so that if the same data or information is needed in next operation, you could directly retrieve it from memory instead of it being generated by the application. Caching is similar to storing state objects. However, the storing information in state objects is deterministic, i.e., you can comfortably count on the data being stored there but caching of data is nondeterministic.

   Applying data caching to multiple layers of your cloud architecture will give you the best application performance you will need.

There are three types of caching; they include Edge Caching, Application Data Caching and Distributed Caching.

- Edge caching: With this, contents are served by infrastructures that are closer to the viewers lowering latency and also offer you the high, sustained data transfer you will need to deliver large popular objects to end users at scale.
- Application data caching: Application data caching will help your application load faster and give your users a better experience. With this, information can be stored and retrieved from fast, managed, in-memory caches in the application, and this decreases load for the database and increases the latency for end-users as mentioned earlier, that caching of data is non-deterministic. The data will not be available in the following cases:
    - If the lifetime of the data expires,
    - If the application releases its memory,
    - If the caching process does not take place for some reasons.

  The primary reason for caching is to reduce the cost of data access, and this can mean either: Monetary costs, for example, paying for the volume of data sent or bandwidth, or Opportunity costs, like processing time that could be used for other purposes.

- Distributed Caching: This is mainly used to store application data residing in database and web session data. Several high volume systems like Google, Amazon, YouTube and many others make use of this technique. This technique allows the web servers to pull and store from distributed server's memory. When this technique is applied, it will enable the web server to simply serve pages without the fear of running out of memory. It will allow the distributed cache to be made up of a cluster of cheaper machines only serving up memory. Once the cluster is set up, you can add a new machine of memory at any time without disrupting your users.

  Have you ever wondered how large companies like Google could return results so quickly,

  When they have thousands of sequential users? Well, this is because they use Clustered Distributed Caching along with other methods to infinitely store the data in memory because memory retrieval is faster than file or DB retrieval.

10. Make sure you remove the single point of failure: Systems are highly available when they can withstand the failure of an individual or multiple components like hard disks, servers, network links etc.

The following processes will guide you through automating the recovery and reducing disruption at every layer of your cloud architecture:

- Introduce redundancy - This will have you remove single points of failure by having multiple resources for the same task. Redundancy can be implemented in either standby mode or active mode. With the standby mode, Functionality is recovered through failover while the resources remain unavailable. While in the active mode, requests are distributed to multiple redundant compute resources. If one of them eventually fails, the rest of them can simply absorb a larger share of the workload.
- Both Identification and reaction to failure should be automated as much as possible.
- It is imperative to have a durable data storage that protects both the availability of data and integrity. Redundant copies of data can be introduced by either synchronous, asynchronous or Quorum based replication.

11. Think Elastic and Adaptive: Cloud architecture is expected to support the growth of users or data size with no drop in performance because there will be growth in these areas. The cloud architecture should also allow for linear scalability when and where an additional resource is added.

Your design should be equipped to take advantage of the virtually unlimited on-demand capacity of cloud computing.

For instance, if you are building cloud architecture for short term purpose, you can implement vertical scaling. If the vertical scaling is not applied, you will need to distribute your workload to multiple resources to build internet-scale applications by scaling horizontally. Either way, your cloud architecture should be elastic enough to adapt to the demands of cloud computing.

Also, to have your cloud very effective in storage, you should know when to engage stateless applications, stateful applications, stateless components and distributed processing.

CHAPTER SIX - MANAGING AND PROVIDING THE CLOUD SOLUTION INFRASTRUCTURE

Cloud infrastructure is extensive and complex. It refers to the servers, software, network devices, and storage devices that make up the cloud. Cloud infrastructure also includes an abstraction layer that virtualizes resources and presents them to users through application program interfaces and APL - enabled command line or graphic interfaces. It's no different from typical data centre infrastructure except that it's virtualized and consumed over the Internet.

Beyond data centres, cloud computing has been a revolutionary technology trend for businesses of all sizes across virtually every industry, and it's become a core component of a modern ecosystem and application integration strategy. Instead of investing in costly hardware while having to manage and maintain a data centre in-house, companies are turning to cloud providers like Amazon Web Services, Google Cloud, and Microsoft Azure for flexible cloud infrastructure to provide modernized computing, networking, and storage know about cloud computing.

Cloud and storage infrastructure falls into three categories - computing, networking.

Cloud infrastructure management is the setup, configuration, monitoring, and optimization of the components of cloud infrastructure. This cloud infrastructure management happens through a web-based interface. Cloud infrastructure management gives enterprises some level of scalability and consolidates IT resources.

Cloud infrastructure consists of servers, storage devices, network, cloud management software, deployment software, and platform virtualization.

Cloud computing infrastructure components

1. Hypervisor

The hypervisor is a firmware or low-level program that acts as a Virtual Machine Manager. It allows us to share the single physical instance of cloud resources between several tenants.

2. Management Software

It helps to maintain and configure the infrastructure.

3. Deployment Software

It helps to deploy and integrate the application on the cloud.

4. Network

The network is the key component of cloud infrastructure. It allows connecting cloud services over the Internet. It is also possible to deliver the network as a utility over the Internet, which means, the customer can customize the network route and protocol.

5. Server

The server helps to compute the resource sharing and offers other services such as resource allocation and de-allocation, monitoring the resources, providing security etc.

6. Storage

Cloud keeps multiple replicas of storage. If one of the storage resources fails, then it can be extracted from another one, which makes cloud computing more reliable.

7. Infrastructural Constraints

Fundamental constraints that cloud infrastructure should implement are shown in the following diagram:

Cloud Computing Infrastructure Constraints

a. Transparency

Virtualization is the key to share resources in a cloud environment. But it is not possible to satisfy the demand with a single resource or server. Therefore, there must be transparency in resources, load balancing and application, so that we can scale them on demand.

b. Scalability

Scaling up an application delivery solution is not that easy as scaling up an application because it involves configuration overhead or even re-architecting the network. So, an application delivery solution is needed to be scalable, which will require the virtual infrastructure such that resource can be provisioned and de-provisioned easily.

c. Intelligent Monitoring

The application solution delivery will need to be capable of intelligent monitoring, this will help achieve transparency and scalability

d. Security

The mega data centre in the cloud should be securely architected. Also, the control node, an entry point in the mega data centre, needs to be secure.

A managed service is a simple resource that logically represents a service integrated with Service Infrastructure, such as Gmail API and Spanner API. A managed service itself has only two immutable properties, a service name and a producer project, but the implementation of a managed service can provide a wide range of functionality. For example, Cloud Storage API provides planet-scale object storage for millions of developers and enterprises.

A managed service has a set of service consumers, a history of immutable service configurations, and a history of immutable service rollouts. The service configurations referenced by the latest service rollout represents the current state of the service, which covers all aspects of the service, from the display name to metrics definitions to rate limits. For the specification, see google.api.Service.

We will describe how to create and manage your service lifecycles on this page. For more information about service management, see How-to Guides.

Creating a service

To create a service, you need to complete the following steps.

I. Install and initialize Cloud SDK on your computer.

II. Create a dedicated producer project to host your service. A dedicated project provides the best security and isolation for your service. It also allows you to transfer the ownership of your service to another team or even another company.

III. Enable Cloud Billing for your project. To integrate your service with Service Infrastructure, you will depend on several paid Google Cloud products, including the Service Control API, Cloud Logging API, and Cloud Monitoring API.

IV. Prepare a simple service configuration file for your service as folio

V. Run cloud command to create your service by deploying a new service configuration:

Cloud endpoints services deploy endpointsapis.yaml

The service creation process takes about a minute. After that, you should be able to see your service listed on the Endpoints page in Google Cloud Console.

Listing services

To list services in a project, you can use the following command:

cloud endpoints services list --project endpoints

Describing a service

Requirements for Building a Cloud Infrastructure

When building out a cloud strategy, several in-depth steps must be taken to ensure a robust infrastructure.

Requirement 1: Service and Resource Management

A cloud infrastructure virtualizes all components of a data centre. Service management is a measured package of applications and services that end users can easily deploy and manage via public and private cloud vendor. And a simplified tool to outline and gauge services is vital for cloud administrators to market functionality. Service management needs to contain resource maintenance, resource guarantees, billing cycles, and measured regulations. Once deployed, management services should help create policies for data and workflows to make sure it's fully efficient, and processes are delivered to systems in the cloud.

Requirement 2: Data Centre Management Tools Integration

Most data centres utilize a variety of IT tools for systems management, security, provisioning, customer care, billing, and directories, among others. And these work with cloud management services and open APIs to integrate existing operation, administration, maintenance, and provisioning (OAM&P) systems. A modern cloud service should support a data centre's existing infrastructure as well as leveraging advanced software, hardware, and virtualization, and other technology.

Requirement 3: Reporting, Visibility, Reliability, and Security

Data centres need high levels of real-time reporting and visibility capabilities in cloud environments to guarantee compliance, SLAs, security, billing, and chargebacks. Without robust reporting and visibility, managing system performance, customer service, and other processes are nearly impossible. And to be wholly reliable, cloud infrastructures must operate regardless of one or more failing components, to safeguard the cloud, services must ensure data and apps are secure while providing access to those who are authorized.

Requirement 4: Interfaces for Users, Admins, and Developers

Automated deployment and self-service interfaces ease complex cloud services for end-users, helping lower operating costs and deliver adoption. Self-service interfaces offer customers the ability to effectively launch a cloud service by managing their own data centres virtually, designing and driving templates, maintaining virtual storage, networking resources, and utilizing libraries. Administrator interfaces present better visibility to all resources, virtual machines, models, service offers, and various cloud users. And all of these structures integrate by way of APIs for developers.

Advantages of Using Cloud Infrastructure

The arguments in favour of using the cloud are only getting stronger as the technology continues to improve. So, there are some obvious key benefits to migrating to a cloud infrastructure that helps companies streamline business processes.

Cost: First and foremost, the cloud removes or greatly reduces the operating expense of a company setting up and managing its own data centre. Taking on this process begins to add up with all the various hardware, software, servers, energy bills, IT experts, and the updates that come along with this multi-faceted set-up. With cloud infrastructure, a company simply pays for it all to be managed while paying only for as-needed services.

Agility and flexibility: Most cloud service infrastructures are offered as self-managed, where service changes can be made within minutes, this improves the uptime and efficiency of business systems while allowing off-site co-workers and partners to access shared data on mobile devices whenever and wherever. And with a cloud infrastructure managing processes, a company becomes more business-focused than IT-focused.

Security: There's a common misconception that cloud services are generally not secure and that data can easily be compromised. There is some truth in that. However, the risks are often blown out of proportion at least in terms of enterprise-level cloud infrastructure and services. Cloud infrastructure technologies and providers are always improving protection against hackers, viruses, and other data breaches with more robust firewalls, advanced encryption keys, and a hybrid approach that stores sensitive data in a private cloud and other data, even apps, in a public cloud.

Disadvantages of Using Cloud Infrastructure

That being said, not all cloud infrastructures are perfect. And while there are far more advantages, there are still some drawbacks.

Vendor overturns: The cloud is still evolving, albeit improving, a technology that rapidly fluctuates. Meaning, some cloud services companies get it right, and some don't. If a company goes out of business or sees a massive overhaul, that could be destructive to a business that relies on just one infrastructure for its entire database.

Connection reliance: A cloud infrastructure is only as good as its network connection. Therefore, the cloud can't stay afloat without a dependable connection. Any glitches in an internet or intranet connection due to a technical outage or storm mean the cloud goes down along with all the data, software, and applications in it. A reliable network means business promises and SLAs are delivered.

Its service provider generally controls control: Since a company's cloud infrastructure, there are times organizations have limited access to data. And business customers have even less power than they might want, with limited access to applications, data, and tools stored on a server.

Basic Requirements For Effective Cloud Infrastructure Management

THERE ARE BASIC REQUIREMENTS FOR EFFECTIVE CLOUD INFRASTRUCTURE MANAGEMENT

SERVICE MANAGEMENT

Productizing cloud functionality requires administrators to have the right tools for the definition and metering of service offerings. A service offering is a set of applications and services that end-users can consume on both public and private clouds.

Private cloud infrastructure is operated for a single organisation. It can be managed internally or by a third party. Individual cloud systems can provide flexible storage capacity and computing power for different areas of business. Still, they lack the element of management that makes cloud computing an attractive economic model for leveraging IT infrastructure. A service offering should ideally include metering rules, guarantees, resource management, and billing cycles. Service management functionality must have a link to the broader offering repository; this makes it easier for the user to deploy and manage defined services.

Public cloud services are delivered over a network that is open for public use. They can provide rigid storage capacity. With this type of cloud, the public can purchase or lease data storage or computing capacity as needed.

VISIBILITY AND REPORTING

It is one of the key components of cloud infrastructure management. We know that security is among the top, if not the top concern for CIOs when making decisions about moving workloads into the cloud. Without visibility into your data, it's hard if not impossible to troubleshoot, to resolve governance issues and to make sure that security controls are working. So because of that, it becomes impossible to monitor customer service levels, compliance, system performance, and billing. Real-time visibility and monitoring give administrators the ability to manage compliance, security, billing, and other instruments seamlessly. They require high levels of granular visibility and reporting.

From a business perspective, this all makes perfect sense in terms of reducing learning curves and nipping problems in the bud before they become major, revenue-affecting calamities.

But monitoring can also shade into analytics, which can add business value. This means allowing you to detect trends in application performance and behaviour, identify usage patterns, and answers to questions about website performance.

So cloud systems management is not only about keeping an eye on systems and responding to alerts. Like any form of predictive maintenance, as used increasingly by companies in all segments, it's all about enabling the ability to become more customer-focused, more agile and flexible, and cutting the costs of managing infrastructure.

If a cloud provider is not delivering on this front, they're not adding enough value. Adam Evans, Director of Professional Services at Rackspace, advises that organisations, post-migration, build a target operating model that assumes change is the new normal.

"Assume that you will constantly be consuming new technologies, then build better processes to assess and bring them ineffectively, this will help you deliver greater business value from these investments and avoid overburdening yourself with managing the growing cloud sprawl."

INTEGRATION WITH DATA CENTER MANAGEMENT TOOLS

Most times, you will need to integrate new cloud management solutions with components of legacy data centres. Legacy data centres have a variety of tools used for provisioning, billing, customer service, systems management, security, directory, and others. Cloud infrastructure management solutions don't replace these tools. It's, therefore, essential to have APIs that integrate into existing OAM&P (operation, administration, maintenance, and provisioning) systems.

Data management is the spine that connects all segments of the information lifecycle.

Data management refers to the professional practice of constructing and maintaining a framework for ingesting, storing, mining, and archiving data integral to modern business. Data management is the spine that connects all segments of the information lifecycle.

Data management works symbiotically with process management, ensuring that the actions teams take are informed by the cleanest, most current data available—which, today, means tracking changes and trends in real-time. Below is a more in-depth look at the practice, its benefits and challenges, and the best practices for helping your organization get the most out of its business intelligence.

END-USER, DEVELOPER, AND ADMINISTRATOR USER INTERFACES

Self-service portals and deployment models help shield the end-user from the complexity of the cloud, and this helps drive adoption and decreases operating costs since the end-user takes up most management tasks. The user can manage his or her virtual data centre, manage virtual storage, and create and launch templates. The user can also access image libraries and manage the network and compute resources.

Administrators should get a UI that gives them a single-pane view of all cloud resources. They should see virtual machine instances, physical resources, service offerings, templates, and users. Developers should also access all these features through standard APIs.

DYNAMIC RESOURCE AND WORKLOAD MANAGEMENT

The cloud must be resource and workload aware. Then, it will be truly on-demand and elastic and meet SLAs (service level agreements). Cloud computing virtualizes all data centre components. The resultant abstraction requires cloud infrastructure management solutions that can create policies around workload and data management. It ensures maximum performance and efficiency for the applications running in the cloud, and it is particularly essential when systems hit peak demand. The system should dynamically prioritize resources on the fly depending on the enterprises' priorities or various workloads.

Cloud resource management has been a critical factor for cloud data centres development. Many cloud datacentres have problems in understanding and implementing the techniques to manage, allocate and migrate the resources in their premises. The consequences of improper resource management may result in underutilized and wastage of resources which may also result in poor service delivery in these datacentres. Funds like, CPU, memory, Hard disk and servers need to be well identified and managed. In this Paper, Dynamic Resource Management Algorithm (DRMA) shall limit itself in the management of CPU and memory as the resources in cloud data centres. The target is to save those resources which may be underutilized at a particular period. It can be achieved through Implementation of suitable algorithms. Here, Bin packing algorithm can be used whereby the best-fit algorithm is deployed to obtain results and compared to select an appropriate algorithm for efficient use of resources.

Cloud Management Tasks

The cloud provider performs several tasks to ensure the efficient use of cloud resources. Here, we will discuss some of them:

Cloud Management Tasks

Audit System Backups

It is required to audit the backups timely to ensure the restoring of randomly selected files of different users. Backups can be performed in the following ways:

Backing up files by the company, from on-site computers to the disks that reside within the cloud.

Backing up files by the cloud provider.

It is necessary to know if the cloud provider has encrypted the data, who has access to that data and if the backup is taken at different locations. The user must know the details of those locations.

Data Flow of the System

The managers are responsible for developing a diagram describing a detailed process flow. This process flow describes the movement of data belonging to an organization throughout the cloud solution.

Vendor Lock-In Awareness and Solutions

The managers must know the procedure to exit from services of a particular cloud provider. The methods must be defined to enable the cloud managers to export data of an organization from their system to another cloud provider.

Knowing Provider's Security Procedures

The managers should know the security plans of the provider for the following services:

- Multitenant use
- E-commerce processing
- Employee screening
- Encryption policy

Monitoring Capacity Planning and Scaling Capabilities

The managers must know the capacity planning to ensure whether the cloud provider is meeting the future capacity requirement for his business or not.

The managers must manage the scaling capabilities to ensure services can be scaled up or down as per the user need.

Monitor Audit Log Use

To identify errors in the system, managers must audit the logs regularly.

Solution Testing and Validation

When the cloud provider provides a solution, it is necessary to test it to ensure that it gives the correct result and it is error-free, this is necessary for a system to be robust and reliable.

CHAPTER SEVEN - SECURITY DESIGN AND COMPLIANCE FOR CLOUD SOLUTION

Introduction

Security Architecture and Design talks about fundamental logical hardware, operating system, and software security components and how to use those components to architect, design, and evaluate secure computer systems. Understanding these fundamental issues is reproving for an information security professional.

Cloud compliance is all about complying with the rules and regulations that apply to use the cloud. Most organizations are moving to the cloud because there are more advantages and benefits to do so. The law does not prevent the adoption of the cloud. It does, however, have a significant impact. When moving to the cloud, it is essential to know in which countries your data will be processed; what laws will apply, what impact they will have, and then follow a risk-based approach to comply with them, this can be very difficult because there are many different kinds of laws, like data localization law, data protection law and data sovereignty laws. You also need to consider interception laws or access to information laws, which may enable Governments or others to access your data in the cloud. Also, the laws of many different countries might apply. It is also essential to know what security measures the law requires you to put in place.

We will just go ahead to look into the different features of how google cloud handles their security designs for cloud infrastructure.

Google security for physical speculation

Google designs and builds its own data centres, which incorporate multiple layers of physical security protections. Access to these data centres is limited to only a tiny fraction of Google employees. They use numerous physical security layers to protect our data centre floors and use technologies like biometric identification, metal detection, cameras, vehicle barriers, and laser-based intrusion detection systems. Google additionally hosts some servers in third-party data centres, where we ensure that there are Google-controlled physical security measures on top of the security layers provided by the data centre operator. For example, in such sites, we may operate independent biometric identification systems, cameras, and metal detectors.

Hardware Design

A Google data centre consists of thousands of server machines connected to a local network. Both the server boards and the networking equipment are custom-designed by Google. They choose component vendors they work with and choose components with care while working with vendors to audit and confirm the security operations which is provided by the components. They also design custom chips, including a hardware security chip that is currently being deployed on both servers and peripherals. These chips allow us to securely identify and authenticate legitimate Google devices at the hardware level.

Secure Boot Stack and Machine Identity

Google server machines use a variety of technologies to ensure that they are booting the correct software stack. We use cryptographic signatures over low-level components like the BIOS, bootloader, kernel, and base operating system image. These signatures can be validated during each boot or update. The components are all Google-controlled, built, and hardened. With each new generation of hardware, we strive to improve security continually: for example, depending on the age of server design, we root the trust of the boot chain in either a lockable firmware chip, a microcontroller running Google-written security code, or the above mentioned Google-designed security chip.

Each server machine in the data centre has its own specific identity that can be tied to the hardware root of trust and the software with which the machine booted. This identity is used to authenticate API calls to and from low-level management services on the machine.

Google has authored automated systems to ensure servers run up-to-date versions of their software stacks (including security patches), to detect and diagnose hardware and software problems, and to remove machines from service if necessary.

Secure Service Deployment

We will now go on to describe how we go from the base hardware and software to ensuring that a service is deployed securely on our infrastructure. By 'service' we mean an application binary that a developer wrote and wants to run on our infrastructure, for example, a Gmail SMTP server, a Bigtable storage server, a YouTube video transcoder, or an App Engine sandbox running a customer application. There may be thousands of machines running copies of the same service to handle the required scale of the workload. Services running on the infrastructure are controlled by a cluster orchestration service called Borg.

As we will see in this section, google infrastructure does not assume any trust between services running on the infrastructure. In other words, the infrastructure is fundamentally designed to be multi-tenant.

Service Identity, Integrity, and Isolation

We use cryptographic authentication and authorization at the application layer for inter-service communication. Provides substantial access control at an abstraction level and granularity that administrators and services can naturally understand.

We do not rely on internal network segmentation or firewalling as our primary security mechanisms. However, we do use ingress and egress filtering at various points in our network to prevent IP spoofing as a further security layer. This approach also helps us to maximize our network's performance and availability.

Each service that runs on the infrastructure has an associated service account identity. Service is provided cryptographic credentials that it can use to prove its identity when making or receiving remote procedure calls (RPCs) to other services. These identities are used by clients to ensure that they are talking to the correct intended server, and by servers to limit access to methods and data to particular clients.

Google's source code is stored in a central repository where both current and past versions of the service are auditable. The infrastructure can additionally be configured to require that a service's binaries be built from specific reviewed, checked in, and tested source code. Such code reviews require inspection and approval from at least one engineer other than the author, and the system enforces that the owners must approve code modifications to any system of that system. These requirements limit the ability of an insider or adversary to make malicious modifications to source code and also provide a forensic trail from service back to its source.

They have a different species of isolation and sandboxing techniques for protecting a service from other services running on the same machine. These techniques include normal separation, language and kernel-based sandboxes, and hardware virtualization. In general, they use more layers of isolation for riskier workloads; for example, when running complex file format converters on user-supplied data or when running user-supplied code for products like Google App Engine or Google Compute Engine. As an extra security boundary, we enable very sensitive services, such as the cluster orchestration service and some key management services, to run exclusively on dedicated machines.

Inter-Service Access Management

The owner of a service can use access management features provided by the infrastructure to specify precisely which other services can communicate with it. For example, a service may want to offer some APIs solely to a specific whitelist of other services. That service can be configured with the whitelist of the allowed service account identities, and this access restriction is then automatically enforced by the infrastructure.

Google engineers accessing services are also issued individual identities, so services can be similarly configured to allow or deny their accesses. All of these types of identities (machine, service, and employee) are in a global namespace that the infrastructure maintains. As will be explained later in this document, end-user identities are handled separately.

The infrastructure provides a productive identity management workflow system for these internal identities, including approval chains, logging, and notification. For example, these identities can be assigned to access control groups via a system that allows two party-controls where one engineer can propose a change to a group that another engineer (who is also an administrator of the group) must approve. This system allows secure access management processes to scale to the thousands of services running on the infrastructure.

In addition to the automatic API-level access control mechanism, the infrastructure also provides services with the ability to read from central ACL and group databases so that they can implement their custom, fine-grained access control where necessary.

Encryption of Inter-Service Communication

Beyond the RPC authentication and authorization capabilities discussed in the previous sections, the infrastructure also provides cryptographic privacy and integrity for RPC data on the network. To give these security benefits to other application layer protocols such as HTTP, we encapsulate them inside our infrastructure RPC mechanisms. In essence, this provides application layer isolation and removes any dependency on the security of the network path. Encrypted inter-service communication can remain secure even if the network is tapped or a network device is compromised.

Services can restructure the level of cryptographic protection they want for each infrastructure RPC (e.g. only configure integrity-level protection for low-value data inside data centres). To protect against sophisticated adversaries who may be trying to tap our private WAN links, the infrastructure automatically encrypts all infrastructure RPC traffic which goes over the WAN between data centres, without requiring any explicit configuration from the service. We have started to deploy hardware cryptographic accelerators that will allow us to extend this default encryption to all infrastructure RPC traffic inside our data centres.

Access Management of End User Data

A typical Google service is written to do something for an end-user. For example, an end-user may store their email on Gmail. The end user's interaction with an application like Gmail spans other services within the infrastructure. So, for example, the Gmail service may call an API provided by the Contacts service to access the end user's address book.

We have seen in the preceding section that the Contacts service can be configured such that the only RPC requests that are allowed are from the Gmail service (or from any other particular services that the Contacts service wants to enable). However, this is still an extensive set of permissions. Within the scope of this permission, the Gmail service would be able to request the contacts of any user at any time.

Since the Gmail service makes an RPC request to the Contacts service on behalf of a particular end-user, the infrastructure provides a capability for the Gmail service to present an "end-user permission ticket" as part of the RPC. This ticket proves that the Gmail service is currently servicing a request on behalf of that particular end-user, this enables the Contacts service to implement a safeguard where it only returns data for the end-user named in the ticket.

The infrastructure provides a central user identity service which issues these "end-user permission tickets." An end-user login is verified by the central identity service which then issues a user credential, such as a cookie or OAuth token, to the user's client device. Every subsequent request from the client device into Google needs to present that user credential.

When a service receives an end-user credential, it passes the credential to the central identity service for verification. If the end-user credential verifies correctly, the central identity service returns a short-lived "end-user permission ticket" that can be used for RPCs related to the request. In our example, that service which gets the "end-user permission ticket" would be the Gmail service, which would pass it to the Contacts service. From that point on, for any cascading calls, the "end-user permission ticket" can be handed down by the calling service to the callee as a part of the RPC call.

Services interact in identity and authentication process.

Service identity and access management: The infrastructure provides service identity, automatic mutual authentication, encrypted inter-service communication and enforcement of access policies defined by the service owner.

Secure Data Storage

Up to this point in the discussion, we have described how we deploy services securely. We will now turn to discuss how we implement secure data storage on the infrastructure.

Encryption at Rest

Google's infrastructure provides a variety of storage services, such as Bigtable and Spanner, and central essential management service. Most applications at Google access physical storage indirectly via these storage services. The storage services can be configured to use keys from the primary key management service to encrypt data before it is written to physical storage. This key management service supports automatic key rotation, provides extensive audit logs, and integrates with the previously mentioned end-user permission tickets to link keys to particular end users.

Performing encryption at the application layer allows the infrastructure to isolate itself from potential threats at the lower levels of storage such as malicious disk firmware. That said, the foundation also implements additional layers of protection. We enable hardware encryption support in our hard drives and SSDs and meticulously track each drive through its lifecycle. Before a decommissioned encrypted storage device can physically leave our custody, it is cleaned using a multi-step process that includes two independent verifications.

Deletion of Data

Deletion of data at Google most often start with marking specific data as "scheduled for deletion" rather than removing the data entirely, and it allows us to recover from unintentional deletions, whether customer-initiated or due to a bug or process error internally. After having been marked as "scheduled for deletion," the data is deleted following service-specific policies.

When an end-user deletes their entire account, the infrastructure notifies services that are handling end-user data that the account has been deleted. The services can then schedule data associated with the deleted end-user account for deletion. This feature enables the developer of service to implement the end-user control quickly.

Secure Internet Communication

Until this point in this document, we have described how we secure services on our infrastructure. In this section, we turn to explain how we ensure communication between the internet and these services.

As discussed earlier, the infrastructure consists of a large set of physical machines which are connected over the LAN and WAN and the security of inter-service communication is not dependent on the security of the network. However, we do isolate our infrastructure from the internet into a private IP space so that we can more easily implement additional protections such as defences against denial of service (DoS) attacks by only exposing a subset of the machines directly to external internet traffic.

Google Front End Service

When a service wants to make itself available on the Internet, it can register itself with an infrastructure service called the Google Front End (GFE). The GFE ensures that all TLS connections are terminated using correct certificates and following best practices such as supporting perfect forward secrecy. The GFE additionally applies protections against

Denial of Service attacks (which we will discuss in more detail later). The GFE then forwards requests for the service using the RPC security protocol discussed previously.

In effect, any internal service which chooses to publish itself externally uses the GFE as a smart reverse-proxy front end. This front end provides public IP hosting of its public DNS name, Denial of Service (DoS) protection, and TLS termination. Note that GFEs run on the infrastructure like any other service and thus have the ability to scale to match incoming request volumes.

Denial of Service (DoS) Protection

The sheer scale of our infrastructure enables Google to absorb many DoS attacks simply. That said, we have multi-tier, multi-layer DoS protections that further reduce the risk of any DoS impact on a service running behind a GFE.

After their backbone delivers an external connection to one of our data centres, it passes through several layers of hardware and software load-balancing. These load balancers report information about incoming traffic to a central DoS service running on the infrastructure. When the central DoS service detects that a DoS attack is taking place, it can configure the load balancers to drop or throttle traffic associated with the attack.

At the next layer, the GFE instances also report information about requests that they are receiving to the central DoS service, including application layer information that the load balancers don't have. The central DoS service can then also configure the GFE instances to drop or throttle attack traffic.

User Authentication

After DoS protection, the next step of defence comes from our central identity service. This service usually manifests to end users as the Google login page. Beyond asking for a simple username and password, the service also intelligently challenges users for additional information based on risk factors such as whether they have logged in from the same device or a similar location in the past. After authenticating the user, the identity service issues credentials such as cookies and OAuth tokens that can be used for subsequent calls.

Users also have the option of employing second factors such as OTPs or phishing-resistant Security Keys when signing in. To ensure that the benefits go beyond Google, they have worked in the FIDO Alliance with multiple device vendors to develop the Universal 2nd Factor (U2F) open standard. These devices are now available in the market, and other primary web services also have followed Google in implementing U2F support.

Operational Security

Up to this point, we have described how security is designed into our infrastructure and have also described some of the mechanisms for secure operation such as access controls on RPCs.

They turn to describe how Google operates the infrastructure securely: they create infrastructure software securely, we protect our employees' machines and credentials, and they defend against threats to the infrastructure from both insiders and external actors.

Safe Software Development

Beyond the central source control and two-party review features described earlier, they also provide libraries that prevent developers from introducing certain classes of security bugs. For example, they have libraries and frameworks that eliminate XSS vulnerabilities in web apps. We also have automated tools for automatically detecting security bugs, including fuzzers, static analysis tools, and web security scanners.

As a final check, we use manual security reviews that range from quick triages for less risky features to in-depth design and implementation reviews for the most dangerous features. These reviews are conducted by a team that includes experts across web security, cryptography, and operating system security. The reports can also result in new security library features and new fuzzers that can then be applied to other future products.

We also run a Vulnerability Rewards Program where we pay anyone who can discover and inform us of bugs in our infrastructure or applications. They have been able to pay several million dollars to people who been able to help them achieve this.

Google also invests a large amount of effort in finding 0-day exploits and other security issues in all the open-source software we use and upstreaming these issues. For example, the OpenSSL Heartbleed bug was found at Google, and we are the largest submitter of CVEs and security bug fixes for the Linux KVM hypervisor.

Keeping Employee Devices and Credentials Safe

We make a massive investment in protecting our employees' devices and credentials from compromise and also in monitoring activity to discover potential compromises or illicit insider activity, this is a critical part of google investment in ensuring that our infrastructure is operated safely.

Reducing Insider Risk

We aggressively limit and actively monitor the activities of employees who have been granted administrative access to the infrastructure and continually work to eliminate the need for privileged access for particular tasks by providing automation that can accomplish the same tasks in a safe and controlled way, this includes requiring two-party approvals for some actions and introducing limited APIs that allow debugging without exposing sensitive information.

Google employee access to end-user information can be logged through low-level infrastructure hooks. Google's security team actively monitors access patterns and investigates unusual events.

Securing Google Cloud

In this section, we highlight how our public cloud infrastructure, Google Cloud, benefits from the security of the underlying infrastructure. In this section, we will take Google Compute Engine as an example service and describe in detail the service-specific security improvements that we build on top of the infrastructure.

Computer Engine enables customers to run their virtual machines on Google's infrastructure. The Compute Engine implementation consists of several logical components, most notably the management control plane and the virtual machines themselves.

The management control plane exposes the external API surface and orchestrates tasks like virtual machine creation and migration. It runs as a variety of services on the infrastructure. Thus it automatically gets foundational integrity features such as a secure boot chain. The individual services run under distinct internal service accounts so that every service can be granted only the permissions it requires when making remote procedure calls (RPCs) to the rest of the control plane. As discussed earlier, the code for all of these services is stored in the central Google source code repository, and there is an audit trail between this code and the binaries that are eventually deployed.

End-user authentication to the Compute Engine control plane API is done via Google's centralized identity service, which provides security features such as hijacking detection. Authorization is done using the central Identity and Access Management service.

The network traffic for the control plane, both from the GFEs to the first service behind it and between other control plane services is automatically authenticated by the infrastructure and encrypted whenever it travels from one data centre to another. Additionally, the infrastructure has been configured to encrypt some of the control plane traffic within the data centre as well.

Compute Engine persistent disks are encrypted at-rest using keys protected by the central infrastructure key management system. It allows for automated rotation and central auditing of access to these keys.

Customers today have the choice of whether to send traffic from their VMs to other VMs or the internet in the clear or to implement any encryption they choose for this traffic. We have started rolling out automatic encryption for the WAN traversal hop of customer VM to VM traffic. As described earlier, all control plane WAN traffic within the infrastructure is already encrypted. In the future, we plan to take advantage of the hardware-accelerated network encryption discussed earlier also to encrypt inter-VM LAN traffic within the data centre.

The isolation provided to the VMs is based on hardware virtualization using the open-source KVM stack. We have further hardened our particular implementation of KVM by moving some of the control and hardware emulation stack into an unprivileged process outside the kernel. We have also extensively tested the core of KVM using techniques like fuzzing, static analysis, and manual code review. As mentioned earlier, the majority of the recent publicly disclosed vulnerabilities which have been upstreamed into KVM came from Google.

Finally, google operational security controls are an essential part of making sure that accesses to data follow our policies. As part of Google Cloud, Compute Engine's use of customer data supports Google Cloud's use of customer data policy, namely that Google will not access or use customer data, except as necessary to provide services to customers.

CHAPTER EIGHT- HOW TO ENSURE SOLUTION AND OPERATION RELIABILITY OF CLOUD ARCHITECTURE

Introduction To The Reliability Of Cloud Architecture

The information has a very serious role to play in the understanding of reliability. Without the right information, achieving the aim of security in cloud architecture would be a far-fetched dream. In reality, no system, plan, strategy or application can be 100 per cent efficient, there's is always be something lacking. If there were a 100 per cent efficient system, there would be the need to discuss this. In every system, certain precautions must be taken to guarantee certain things. Specific steps must be observed. And so, in the case of Cloud architecture, the same principle applies.

Reliability comes into play in the place of inefficiency. When looking out for an excellent system to work with, do we check and base solely on its efficiency? It would be wrong because the system could be "100 per cent efficient" ideally speaking, but no accurate test for reliability can keep it working. Security, therefore, is agreeably important in anything we work towards and should be applied in this line of action.

On this note, for reliability to stand out, there must be specific parameters that must be met through series of tests, that could as well correlate with past data to keep the solution and operation of a cloud architecture reliable and worthile to be used. It is important to note that ensuring the reliability of an application, platform, or cloud architecture will make other features they have evidence to the users.

Before we proceed in exploring the methodology behind ensuring the solution and reliability of cloud architecture, let us examine what the word "reliable" and "reliability" means. According to the Merriam Webster dictionary, we have the following definitions for "reliable":

* Able to be trusted to do or provide what is needed; able to be relied on; ready to be believed; likely to be accurate or correct
* Suitable or fit to be relied on- dependable.
* Giving the same result on successive trials

While RELIABILITY means: the quality or state of being reliable; the extent to which an experiment, test, or measuring procedure yields the same results on repeated trials.

From the definitions above, it should be noted that reliability speaks of continuous and progressive development. It is something that lives on with time. Hence, whatever measures one must employ to ensure security has to have a continuity effect. As this is the aim of this section, there is an outlined guide for processes that will help achieve reliability goals.

Some key factors to consider while ensuring the reliability of cloud architecture (application or platform) are;

1. Operational techniques involved in running the cloud architecture must require very little manual work and mental load from the operators or users, while at the same time ensuring rapid reduction of the failures accompanying it.
2. Measurable goals considered to be reliable must be set in place, and corrections to deviation from such goals or parameters must be promptly done. This is a pivotal aspect of achieving one's reliability goals. It is therefore desirable that if you must be successful at gaining reliability, you must have to set realistic goals.
3. Flexibility, scalability, availability, and automated change management are to be considered in cloud architecture.
4. Self-healing and observance must be part of the cloud architecture.

Identifier For Cloud Architecture Reliability

In the exploration of the meaning of reliability and its relationship to cloud architecture, there is a necessity to identify the factors that must be considered in the process of achieving security of cloud architecture. These factors are very crucial and should not be taken likely.

These are treated as follows;

1. The User defines Reliability. this deals with the question "what does the user of the cloud architecture consider as reliable?" Now depending on the system your cloud architecture adopts, there are various ways to gather this data, compile it and work with it. In the case of a user-facing workload, measuring the user experience of primary importance, an example is a query success ratio. Many system workloads have different methods of getting the user-defined reliability values needed to determine what could make the cloud architecture designed reliable.

Sufficient Reliability. It is necessary to set Service Level Objectives (SLOs) that will give a reliability threshold and will also use error budgets to manage the rate of change to the cloud architecture. The cloud architecture would thus be reliable but not too secure that it becomes unjustified. Therefore, your SLOs or reliability parameters should be within a range of values

Redundancy. No single points of failure are features of a cloud architecture with high-reliability needs. Resources for reliable cloud architecture are replicated across multiple failure domains. Failure domains are pools of resources that are capable of failing independently.

Horizontal Scalability. Traffic growth or data growth through the addition of more resources should be accommodated in your cloud architecture, and it is essential to include this factor.

Overload Tolerance: This is quite self-explanatory. In case of an overload to the cloud architecture, a useful tolerance feature is essential to avoid crashing of the cloud.

Rollback Capacity. Change is constant and is essential to ensure growth and development of the cloud architecture. However, a method to undo a modification done to the cloud architecture is highly relevant - that is, roll back the difference.

Traffic Control. Countless clients sending traffic to cloud architecture at the same instant can lead to cascading failures as a result of traffic spikes, to control this, it is essential not to synchronize requests across clients.

Test Failure Recovery. Failure recovery is an important feature, but it is essential to test it periodically. If it is not tested, it may not function when you need it. Set failure recovery procedures and test them out regularly. Some methods to test include rolling back a release and restoring data from backups.

Failure Detection. In case of failures in the cloud architecture, a method to detect these failures right on time should be put in place. Alerting too soon and too late is not right, to prevent these, the delay before notification must be set the right possible way.

Incremental Changes. Changes made to the cloud architecture should be done gradually with "canary testing" to detect bugs in the early stages where their impact to users is minimal. Instantaneous global changes are hazardous.

Coordinated Emergency Response. Operational practices that minimize the duration of outages, as well as consider the customer's experience and users well-being should be observed. Hence, advanced formalization of response procedures with well-defined roles and communication channels.

System Observability Feature. The cloud architecture system should be sufficiently developed to enable rapid triaging, troubleshooting, and diagnosis of a problem to minimize outages.

Capacity Management. The cloud architecture should be equipped with the function to give traffic and provision resources in advance of peak traffic events.

Documentation and Automated Emergency Responses. Pre-plan emergency actions, document them and ideally automate and corporate them into the cloud architecture in case of emergencies. People find it difficult in defining what should be done in such situations.

Toil Reduction. "What is toil?" one may ask. Toil is repetitive manual work with no enduring value. It is important to note that toil increases with service growth. Reduction of total elimination of drudgery in the cloud architecture is one of the things to seek out for; otherwise, operational work would become too much for the users, thus leaving little or no room for the successful growth of the cloud architecture.

We have gone a long way in identifying factors and markers that can make cloud architecture reliable. The knowledge of these factors is on one ground, but applying this knowledge in the best way to ensure reliability is another ball game altogether. It is essential to know how to use this knowledge to achieve a successful and reliable cloud architecture since cloud architecture is a significant and crucial component of the currently fast-developing world we live in today.

Ensuring Solution And Operational Reliability Of Cloud Architecture

These are a series of steps or practices as you may like to call them, that must be observed to ensure the proper functioning and reliability of cloud architecture. These include;

Reliability Goal Definition. Existing customer experience, tolerance for errors and mistakes should be accounted for while defining reliability goals. If the data that a user expects from a cloud architecture is not there, then the overall uptime goal of 100 per cent over an infinite amount of time is both meaningless and will not be achieved.

On this note, SLOs based on the user experience should be set; this is carried out successfully by measuring the reliability metrics as close to the user as possible. Measuring reliability at the server should be the last resort for this process. A high SLO that makes the user happy is ideal and no higher than that.

A target lower than 100 per cent for uptime and other vital metrics is strongly advised, although target should be close to 100 per cent. This target allows for fast and quality service.

Reliability goals that are achievable and set according to the customer experience help determine the highest pace and scope of changes that users can tolerate.

Competitive benchmark analysis could be used if existing customer experiences can not be measured. Measure customer experience even if you cannot define goals yet, in case of absence of comparable competition.

SLIs, SLOs and SLAs. Service Level Indicators (SLIs) are quantitative measures of some aspect of the provided level of service. It is a metric and not a target. Service Level Objectives (SLOs) are the targets for the reliability of your cloud architecture. SLOs are very vital in making data-driven decisions about safety; thus, they are the core of SRE practices. SLOs are the values for SLIs, and cloud architecture is considered reliable if the SLIs are at or above this value. Service Level Agreements (SLAs) are contracts with the user, which includes consequences of meeting or missing the stated SLOs; they can be explicit or implicit. It is an excellent practice to have stricter internal SLOs than external SLAs.

Error budgeting helps to manage development velocity of the cloud architecture. Launch new features quickly if the error budget is not yet consumed. However, freeze or slow down changes if the error budget is close to zero, then invest engineering resources into reliability features.

Examples of SLIs

For serving systems, the following SLIs are typical and very important, hence ensure you go through them critically and carefully, to milk the juice therein:

Availability: There's always the question of how possible it is to tell precisely how much fraction of time is required per time in any service; this is where availability comes in to play. One may also ask, "How can I identify this?" this is also covered here. More often than not, this factor is determined and recognized following well-formed requests that succeed—for example, 99% seals the deal.

Latency: On the other hand, if you have ever had concerns on how much time a certain percentage of request could take to be fulfilled, welcome to LANTENCY. It is often defined in terms of percentile other than 50th—for example, 99th percentile at 300 ms.

Quality: At this juncture, you may want to know how much response a specific service has garnered. If this is the case, Quality tells you how good a particular response is. Quality is often defined in terms of specific services, indicating the extent to which the content of the response to a request varies from the ideal response content. Quality here can be two different folds (bad or good) or better still, and we can evaluate quality between the range of 0% to 100%.

For data processing systems, the following SLIs are typical and equally relevant:

Coverage: In a case where you are concerned with the amount of data that has been processed, Coverage tells you the fraction of data that has been processed—for example, 99.9% and so on.

Correctness: For you to be able to determine the responses that are bound to be correct and acceptable, correctness addresses that for you— for example, 99.99%.

Freshness: tells you how latest the data source is, or how much of aggregated responses you have present in your system, the more frequent, the better—for example, 20 minutes.

Throughput: to find out how much data is going through processing, you welcome to Throughput. Therein lies your solution. Thus, Throughput measures the amount of data being processed per time—for example, 500 MiB/sec or even 1000 RPS.

For storage systems, the following SLIs are common:

Durability: As an operator, many cases may arise for you to retrieve data written in the system for future purposes - this is where durability comes in. Durability, therefore, helps you determine your capabilities to access saved write-ups on the system for future uses. Thus, when any data is lost or misplaced from the system, it spells room for your durability metric—for instance, 99.9999%.

Throughput: Throughput tells you how much data is being processed per time.

Latency: Latency talks about the duration used for any request to be fulfilled. It speaks loudly about time measurement.

Incorporate Observability into the Cloud Architecture; this would include monitoring, tracing, logging, debugging, profiling and other methods involved in observing, and this is to ensure the cloud architecture maximizes observability to the fullest. A well-designed cloud architecture strives to have the necessary observability starting with the development phase. Common anti-patterns to avoid are over-engineering monitoring and over-alerting, and this can be achieved by actively deleting time series, dashboards, and alerts not looked at or rarely fired during the initial launch stages.

Design for Scale and high availability. Your cloud architecture needs to be very scalable and readily available. A multi-region architecture with failover should be designed into your cloud architecture if you want it to be available even when an entire region is down. Get rid of single points of failure like a single-region master database as it can cause a global outrage if unreachable. Also, by identifying architecture components that can not grow beyond the resource limits of a single zone and redesigning these components to be horizontally scalable, since such elements have hard limits on their scalability and often require manual reconfiguration to carry outgrowth, you can eliminate scalability bottlenecks. An alternative to redesigning is replacing these components with managed services designed to scale with no user action.

Cloud architecture should be designed in such a way that it would detect overload and return quality responses to the user or partially give traffic rather than failing. Implementing exponential backoff with jitter in your cloud architecture can prevent a generation of instantaneous traffic spikes from large groups of users since these spikes can potentially crash the cloud architecture. However, if the cloud architecture experiences known periods of peak traffic, make sure to prepare for such events adequately to avoid significant loss of revenue and traffic. Finally, do not wait for disasters to strike; periodically test as well as verify your disaster recovery procedures and processes you have put in place in your cloud architecture.

Build-in Flexible and Automated Deployment Capabilities. Redesign the cloud architecture to support rollback and test the rollback processes periodically, if there is no defined way to undo specific changes. Spreading out traffic for time promotions (this includes special events) and launches helps to significantly prevent instantaneous traffic spikes that could crash your cloud architecture at the scheduled start time. Canary system testing alerts one to problems and might even automatically halt rollouts, therefore it is beneficial to implement progressive implementation with canary testing.

Automation is functional and an enormous arsenal added to the design of your cloud architecture, but, it is not a cure, this is because it comes with a fair share of maintenance costs and risks to reliability beyond its initial development and setup costs. Hence, a continuous process of inventorying and assessing the cost of toil on the team managing the cloud architecture is greatly recommended before investing in customized automation.

Efficient Alerting System should be Used. Optimize alerting delay by tuning the configured delay before the monitoring system notifies humans of a problem to minimize outages while maximizing signal versus noise. Set to trigger alerts based on the direct impact on user experiences, which is based on symptoms and not causes.

A Collaborative Incident Management Process Should be built. Failing to meet SLOs is inevitable for any cloud architecture. However, in the absence of an SLO, your customers will still define based on their experience what the acceptable service level is, this will escalate to your technical support or similar group irrespective of the contents of your SLA, to satisfy your users adequately, it is recommended that you establish and regularly implement an incident management plan.

Let us take a few examples of the Incident Management Plan. This part is one of the "bumpy rides" you may encounter; this is where we would draw the curtain in this one.

Example Of Incident Management Plan

* Should I delegate in the first place? Yes, if you and your team can't resolve this.
* Is this a privacy or security breach? If yes, then delegate to the privacy/security team
* Production issues have been detected (alert, page) or escalated to me.
* Should I involve more people? Yes, if it is impacting more than X% of customers or if it takes more than Y minutes to resolve. If in doubt, always involve more people, especially during business hours.
* Attend recurring postmortem incident review meeting to discuss and staff action items.
* Is this an emergency or are SLO(s) at risk? If in doubt, treat it as an emergency
* Define when the incident is over, this might require acknowledgment from a Support representative.
* Define a primary communications channel—for example, IRC, Hangouts Chat, or Slack.

CHAPTER NINE- EXAM GUIDE

Do you want to be a certified Google cloud professional architect or validate your skills to work on cloud technologies? Professional Google Cloud certification exam is the answer. Google cloud architect certification exam is geared towards having significant knowledge of working on Google Cloud. The Google Cloud Certified Professional Cloud Architect Exam Guide is an essential resource for anyone preparing for this highly sought-after, professional-level certification. Detailed explanations of crucial topics include analyzing and defining technical and business processes, migration planning, and designing storage systems, networks, and compute resources.

Providing services suitable for a wide range of applications, particularly in high-growth areas of analytics and machine learning, Google Cloud is rapidly gaining market share in the cloud computing world. Organizations are seeking certified IT professionals with the ability to deploy and operate infrastructure, services, and networks in the Google Cloud. Take your career to the next level by validating your skills and earning certification. The Google Cloud Certified Professional Cloud Architect Exam Guide is a must-have for

IT professionals preparing for certification to deploy and manage Google cloud services

Overview Of Google Cloud Architect Exam

Google Professional Cloud Architect Exam enables individuals and organizations to have the technical knowledge and analytical skills to leverage Google Cloud technologies. With proper knowledge and understanding of the Google cloud and cloud architecture, the organization or individuals involved can, develop designs, manage, secure available and dynamic solutions to set any business objectives in motion. A certified Cloud Architect is an individual who has proficiency in all the aspects of solution design, enterprise cloud strategy and best architectural practices. The certified Cloud Architect should also be able to show a high level of experience with software development methodology and multi-tiered distributed applications which span hybrid or multi-cloud environments. The Professional Cloud Architect exam was set up to assess, to test knowledge of the ability of an individual to plan a cloud solution architecture, manage the cloud solution infrastructure, design (for compliance and security), analyze technical processes, optimize business processes, ensure operations reliability and manage the implementation of cloud architecture.

It is imperative that the exam structure and format be understood before attempting the exam; this is an overview of the Google Cloud Architect Certification exam.

Google cloud architecture is not limited to any range of roles yet, and it is mainly intended for

- Enterprise/solutions architect
- Operations team(members of the operations team)
- System administrators
- Graduates who would like to build a career as cloud architects

When preparing for Google Cloud Architect exam, you must make sure you understand the objectives. Google made it easy to understand by dividing the exam syllabus into various subject areas. Below are the topics that are covered during the exam; this should be your focus during the preparation.

1. Plan and Design a Cloud Solution Architecture

   Design a solution infrastructure that business requirements

   Design a solution infrastructure meeting technical requirements

   Design storage, network, and compute resources

   Create a migration plan

   Envision of the solution improvements for future

2. Provision and Management of Solution Infrastructure

   The configuration of network topologies

   The configuration of individual storage systems

The configuration of computer systems

3. Compliance and Security Design

   Design Security

   Design legal compliance

4. Analyze and Optimize business and technical processes

   Analyze and define technical processes

   Analyze and define business Processes

   Develop procedures for testing solution resilience under production

5. Implementation Management

   Advise operation/development and ensure that solution is implemented successfully

   Read and write the languages for application development

6. Ensure the reliability of solution and operations

   Log, monitor, and alert solution

   Release management and deployment

   Support troubleshooting of operations

   Evaluate different measures for quality control

1. DESIGNING AND PLANNING A CLOUD SOLUTION ARCHITECTURE

To design a solution infrastructure that will meet the requirements of a business, you must consider the following facts:

- Possible cases of business use and the product strategy
- Possible ways of optimizing cost
- Support for the design
- Integration with multi-cloud environments (external systems)
- Movement of data
- Design decision trade-offs
- But, build or modify
- Measurement of success - e.g. key performance indicators
- Observability and compliance

Consider the following facts when designing a solution that should meet technical requirements

- Failover design and high availability
- Cloud resources elasticity
- Ability of the design to be produced in a range of capabilities (ability to meet growth requirements)
- Latency and performance

For designing compute resources, storage and network, consider the following:

- Integration with multi-cloud environments and systems in the premises of the organization (on-premises systems)
- Cloud-native networking
- Choosing data process technologies
- Choosing appropriate storage types
- Choosing compute resources
- Matching the compute needs to the platform products

Consider the following facts when creating a migration plan

- Integrating solutions with already existing systems
- Migrating data and systems to support the solution
- Mapping licencing
- Network planning
- Testing and proof of concept
- Dependency management planning

For envisioning future solution improvements, the following facts should be considered:

- Technology and cloud improvement
- Business evolution
- Advocacy and publicity

2. MANAGING AND PROVIDING A SOLUTION INFRASTRUCTURE

When configuring network topologies, the following should be considered:

- Hybrid networking (extending to systems within the premises of the organization)
- Extending to systems outside the premises of the organization that may include GCP to GCP communication
- Data protection and security

For individual storage system configuration, consider the following:

- Allocation of data storage
- Compute provisioning/data processing
- Access and security management
- Configuration of the network for late cy and data transfer
- Data life cycle management and data retention
- Data growth management

For compute systems, the following should be considered:

- Compute system provisioning
- Configuration of computing volatility
- Configuration of a network for compute nodes

- Configuration of infrastructure provisioning technology, e.g. terraform/deployment manager
- Use of Kubernetes for container orchestration

3. DESIGNING FOR SECURITY ANC COMPLIANCE

Consider the following when designing for security

- IAM – identity and access management
- Resource hierarchy – organizations, folders, projects
- Data security – encryption
- Testing of penetration
- SoD – separation of duties
- Managed encryption keys with cloud KMS – managing customer

Consider these facts when designing for compliance

- Certification of industry
- Audits
- Legislation – data privacy, health record privacy
- Commercial – handling of sensitive data such as credit card information

4. ANALYZING AND OPTIMIZING TECHNICAL AND BUSINESS PROCESSES

Consider the following when analyzing and defining technical processes:

- Life cycle plan of software development

- Continuous deployment/continuous integration
- Post mortem analysis culture (troubleshooting)
- Validation and testing
- Provisioning and service catalogue
- Disaster recovery and business continuity

Consider the following when analyzing and defining business processes:

- Stakeholder management - facilitation and influencing
- Management change
- Skills readiness/team assessment
- Process of decision making
- Management of customer success
- Resource optimization/cost optimization

You should also be able to develop procedures that ensure the resilience of a solution in production

5. MANAGING IMPLEMENTATION

When advising development/operation team to ensure the successful deployment of the solution, consider the following factors:

- API best practices
- Development of application
- Framework testing -integration/unit/load

- System migrating and data tooling

When interacting with Google Cloud using GCP SDK, Consider the following

- Google cloud shell
- Local installation

You must also ensure the reliability of the solution and operations. You can do this by:

- Monitoring/logging/profiling/alerting solution
- Release and deployment management
- Assisting in solution support during operations
- Evaluation of quality control measure

During the Cloud Architect certification exam, some questions may refer you to case studies that describe a fictitious business and solution. These case studies provide additional context that will help you choose your answers. One such case study is:

TerramEarth

It is one of the sample case studies that can be used during the Professional Cloud Architect exam. This case study describes a fictitious business and solution concept, and this helps to provide additional context to the exam questions.

TerramEarth is an industry that manufactures heavy equipment for the agricultural and mining sectors. 20% of their business is from agriculture, and 80% is from mining. They have over 600 service centres and dealers in 100 countries with the mission to build products that will aid their customers to become more productive.

1. SOLUTION CONCEPT

TerramEarthhas 20 million vehicles in operation that gather collect 120 fields of data every second. Data for analysis can be assessed when any of these vehicles have been serviced because data is stored locally on the vehicle. This data is downloaded by a maintenance port which can be used to adjust operational parameters, and this allows the vehicles to be upgraded in the field with new computing modules.TerramEarth can collect data directly from a cellular network which has approximately 200,000 vehicles connected to it. TerramEarth, therefore, collects 9TB per day from these connected vehicles, this is done at a rate of 120 fields every second, with daily operations of 22 hours.

2. EXISTING TECHNICAL ENVIRONMENT

TerramEarth has an existing architecture that is composed of Linux and Windows-based systems that all reside in a U.S west-coast-based data centre. These systems upload files gotten from the field (CSV files) via FTP and store the data in their data warehouse. Aggregated reports are always based on data that is three weeks old because this process takes a lot of time. TerramEarth can preemptively stock replacement parts, spare parts and reduces planned downtime of their work vehicles with the data that is stored in their data warehouse. While they wait for replacement parts, some customers stay without their vehicles for about three to four weeks because the data is stale.

3. BUSINESS REQUIREMENTS

TerramEarth should have the ability to partner with different companies to create a compelling offering for their customers (e.g. seed and fertilizer suppliers in the agricultural business)

They should be able to have and support dealer network with a lot more data on how their customers use their equipment to better position new products and services

They should be able to decrease the downtime of vehicles to less than one week.

4. TECHNICAL REQUIREMENTS

Improvement of data in their data warehouse

Increase the security of transfer of data from the equipment to the data centre

Ability to use equipment and customer data to predict customer needs

Ability to create a backup strategy

Expansion beyond a single data centre

5. APPLICATION 1: DATA INGESTION

Here a Python application reads the uploaded files gotten from a single server and writes to their data warehouse

Compute:

Windows Server 2008 R2

16 CPUs

128GB of RAM

10 TB of local HDD storage

6. APPLICATION 2: REPORTING

It is an application (off the shelf) that is used by business analysts to run a daily check to see the equipment that needs repair. This application is limited to two analysts at a time.

Compute

Application. License tied to the number of physical CPUs

Windows Server 2008 R2

16 CPUs

32 GB RAM

500 GB HDD

Data warehouse

A single PostgreSQL server

RedHat Linux

64 CPUs

128 GB RAM

4x 6TB HDD in RAID O

7. EXECUTIVE STATEMENT

Our ability to build better vehicles for lower costs than our competitors has always been our competitive advantage in our manufacturing process. Even though I'm concerned that we lack the skills to undergo the next of transformations in our industry, new products with different approaches and styles are continually being developed. While addressing an immediate market need through incremental innovations, our goals are to build more skills which will help us harness the new waves of transformation.

Other examples of fictitious case studies are Mountkirk Games and Dress4win

MOUNTKIRK GAMES

Mountkirk Games makes online, multiplayer, session-based games for mobile platforms. All their games are built using server-side integration. Historically, they have used cloud providers to lease physical servers. They have had to face problems such as scaling their global audience, application servers, MySQL databases, and analytics tools, due to the unexpected popularity of some of their games.

To be able to scale their problems, their current model is to write game statistics to files and send them through an ETL tool that loads them into a centralized MySQL database for reporting.

1. Solution concept

Mountkirk Games is building a new game, which they expect to be very popular. To be able to capture streaming metrics, carry out intensive analytics and also take advantage of its auto-scaling server environment and integrate with a managed NoSQL database they plan to deploy the game's backend on Compute Engine

2. Business requirements

Increase to a global footprint

Reduce latency to all customers

Improve uptime because downtime is the loss of players

Increase the efficiency of the cloud resources used

3. TECHNICAL REQUIREMENTS

Requirements for game backend platform

Based on game activity, dynamically scale up or down

Connect to a transactional database service to manage user profiles and game state

Storage of game activity in a time series database service for future analysis

Ensure that data is not lost due to processing backlogs as the system scales

Run hardened Linux distro

Requirements for game analytics platform

Dynamically scale up or down based on game activity

Process incoming data on the fly directly from the game servers

Process data that arrives late because of slow mobile networks

Allow queries to access at least 10 TB of historical data

Process files that are regularly uploaded by users' mobile devices

4. EXECUTIVE STATEMENT

Our last successful game had low user adoption, and this affected the game's reputation because it did not scale well with our previous cloud provider. To evaluate the speed and stability of the game, as well as other metrics that provide more in-depth insight into usage patterns so we can adapt the game to target users, our investors want more key performance indicators (KPIs). Additionally, we want to replace MySQL and move to an environment that provides auto-scaling and low latency load balancing and frees us up from managing physical servers because our current technology stack cannot provide the scale we need.

DRESS4WIN

Dress4Win is a web-based company that helps its users manage and organize their wardrobe using a web app and mobile application. They monetize their services through advertising, ecommerce, referrals, and a freemium app model. The company also cultivates an active social network that connects its users with designers and retailers. The application has grown from a few servers in the founder's garage to several hundred servers and appliances in a collocated data centre. However, because of the increase in users, their infrastructure capacity is now insufficient. Dress4Win is committing to a full migration to a public cloud because of its rapid growth and the company's desire to innovate faster

1. SOLUTION CONCEPT

Dress4Win is moving their development and test environments for the first phase of their migration to the cloud. Because of their current infrastructure at a single location, they are also building a disaster recovery site. They are not sure which components of their architecture they can migrate as is and which elements they need to change before migrating them.

2. EXISTING TECHNICAL ENVIRONMENT

As earlier stated, the Dress4Win application is served out of a single data centre location. All servers run Ubuntu LTS v16.04.

Databases:

MySQL. One server for user data, inventory, static data,

MySQL 5.7

8 core CPUs

128 GB of RAM

2x 5 TB HDD (RAID 1)

Compute:

40 web application servers providing micro-services based APIs and static content

Tomcat – Java

Nginx

Four core CPUs

32 GB of RAM

20 Apache Hadoop/Spark servers:

Data analysis

Real-time trending calculations

Eight core CPUs

128 GB of RAM

4x 5 TB HDD (RAID 1)

Three RabbitMQ servers for messaging, social notifications, and events:

Eight core CPUs

32GB of RAM

Different servers:

Jenkins, monitoring, bastion hosts, security scanners

Eight core CPUs

32GB of RAM

Storage appliances:
iSCSI for VM hosts

Fibre channel SAN – MySQL databases

1 PB total storage; 400 TB available

NAS – image storage, logs, backups

100 TB total storage; 35 TB available

3. BUSINESS REQUIREMENT

The building of a reproducible and reliable environment with scaled parity of production.

Adhering to a set of security and identity, access management best practices to improve security

Improve business agility and speed of innovation through rapid provisioning of new resources

Analyze and optimize architecture for better performance in the cloud

4. TECHNICAL REQUIREMENTS

Easily create non-production environments in the cloud

Provisioning resources in the cloud by the implementation of an automation framework

Deploying applications to the on-premises data cloud or centre by the implementation of a continuous deployment process

Support failover of the production environment to cloud during an emergency

Encrypt data on the wire and at rest

Support multiple private connections between the production data centre and cloud environment.

5. EXECUTIVE STATEMENT

Our investors are concerned that a competitor could use a public cloud platform to offset their up-front investment and free them so that they can focus on the development of better features. They are also concerned about our ability to contain costs and scale with our current infrastructure. 80% of our capacity is sitting idle while at other times our traffic patterns are highest in the mornings and weekend evenings.

Our capital expenditure is now exceeding our quarterly projections. Migrating to the cloud will likely cause an initial increase in spending, but we expect to transition before our next hardware refresh cycle fully. Our total cost of ownership (TCO) analysis over the next five years for a public cloud strategy achieves a cost reduction between 30% and 50% over our current model.

SUMMARY

The Google Cloud Professional Architect exam covers a lot of broad areas including the

- Planning of cloud solutions
- Managing of cloud solutions
- The Securing of systems and process
- Complying with industry and government regulations and rules
- Maintenance of solutions deployed for production and monitoring of the application
- Understanding of technical and business requirements and considerations

All these areas require both business and technical skills. For example, Architects need to understand issues such as accelerating the pace of development, maintaining and reporting on the service-level agreement, reducing operational expenses and assisting with regulatory compliance, since they regularly work with non-technical colleagues. In the realm of technical knowledge, architects are expected to understand functional requirements around computing, storage and networking as well as non-functional requirements of service such as availability and scalability. Some exam questions reference the case studies.

CHAPTER TEN - PROFESSIONAL CLOUD ARCHITECT EXAM

The Professional Cloud Architect practice exam will help familiarize you with the types of questions you will encounter during the certification exam. It will also help you tell your level of readiness and inform you if there will be a need for more preparation and practical experience.

The successful completion of this practice exam does not in any way guarantee that you will pass the certification exam. Reasons being that the actual exam takes longer time and covers a broader range of topics. You are advised to refer to the exam guide for a list of topics you could use for a test.

* A company was planning to migrate their on-premises Microsoft SQL server to Google Cloud with minimal efforts. They want to set up a high availability solution across zones. How do you set up the high availability for the database?

A. Migrate the Microsoft SQL Server to Cloud Spanner, as it is distributed globally

B. Create a Read Replica for the Microsoft SQL Server and configure for its failover

C. Use Windows Server Failover Clustering and SQL Server Always On Availability Groups

D. Migrate to Cloud SQL and enable automatic failover

* A company is planning to host its critical application on Google Cloud and wants to ensure that the application will handle the load even if an entire zone fails. What two options would you recommend?

A. Don't select the "Multi-zone" option when creating your managed instance group.

B. Spread your managed instance group over two zones and overprovision by 100%. (for Two Zone)

C. Create a regional unmanaged instance group and spread your instances across multiple zones.

D. Overprovision your regional managed instance group by at least 50%. (for Three Zones)

* A Company is planning the migration of their web application to Google App Engine. However, they would continue to use their on-premises database. How can they set up application?

A. Setup the application using App Engine Standard environment with Cloud VPN to connect to database

B. Setup the application using App Engine Flexible environment with Cloud VPN to connect to database

C. Setup the application using App Engine Standard environment with Cloud Router to connect to database

D. Setup the application using App Engine Flexible environment with Cloud Router to connect to d

* A company is migrating its data to Google Cloud using Cloud VPN tunnel. They are trying to set up Virtual Private Network on Cloud Which of the following conditions is true regarding the IPs?

A. Primary IPs between on-premises and Cloud should not overlap, while Secondary IPs can overlap

B. Primary & Secondary IPs between on-premises and Cloud can overlap

C. Primary IPs between on-premises and Cloud can overlap, while Secondary IPs should not overlap

D. Primary & Secondary IPs between on-premises and Cloud should not overlap

* A company is hosting its web hosting platform on Google Cloud using Google Kubernetes Engine. The application now needs to credit payments and needs to be PCI-DSS compliant. How can the company handle the requirement?

A. As GCP is PCI-DSS complaint, there is no separate handling for individual services

B. GKE is not PCI-DSS compliant as services run on shared hosts, and the requirement cannot be fulfilled

C. GKE and GCP provides you with tools to handle PCI-DSS compliance

D. GKE is PCI-DSS complaint, and no additional changes are

* A company hosts their applications on Google Cloud. They handle PII data and want to protect PII sensitive data like email, address, phone number, credit card before the data is stored on their system for analysis. How should the company handle the same?

A. Perform hashing of PII data using SHA256

B. De-identify the data using Data loss prevention API

C. Perform data encryption using cyclic encryption

D. Configure regex patterns to handle all the PII data and perform redaction.

* A company has a lot of data sources from multiple systems used for reporting. Over a while, a lot of data is missing, and you are asked to perform anomaly detection. How would you design the system?

A. Use Dataprep with Data Studio

B. Load in Cloud Storage and use Dataflow with Data Studio

C. Load in Cloud Storage and use Dataprep with Data Studio

D. Use Dataflow with Data Studio

* A client wants to store files from one location and retrieve them from another location. Security requirements are that no one should be able to access the contents of the file while it is hosted in the cloud. What is the best option?

A. Default encryption should be sufficient

B. Customer-Supplied Encryption Keys (CSEK)

C. Customer Managed Encryption Keys (CMEK)

D. Client-side encryption

* A client is using Cloud SQL database to serve infrequently changing lookup tables that host data used by applications. The applications will not modify the tables. As they expand into other geographic regions, they want to ensure excellent performance. What do you recommend?

A. Migrate to Cloud Spanner

B. Read replicas

C. Instance high availability configuration

D. Migrate to Cloud Storage

* Your customer is moving their storage product to Google Cloud Storage (GCS). The data contains personally identifiable information (PII) and sensitive customer information. What security strategy should you use for GCS?

A. Use signed URLs to generate time-bound access to objects.

B. Grant IAM read-only access to users, and use default ACLs on the bucket.

C. Grant no Google Cloud Identity and Access Management (Cloud IAM) roles to users, and use granular ACLs on the bucket.

D. Create randomized bucket and object names. Enable public access, but only provide specific file URLs to people who do not have Google accounts and need access

* Your company wants to track whether someone is present in a meeting room reserved for a scheduled meeting. There are 1000 meeting grooms across five offices on three continents. Each room is equipped with a motion sensor that reports its status every second. The data from the motion detector includes only a sensor ID and several different discrete items of information. Analysts will use this data, together with information about account owners and office locations. Which database type should you use?

A. Flat file

B. NoSQL

C. Relational

D. Blobstore

CHAPTER ELEVEN - CONCLUSION

Google Cloud's Architecture Framework describes best practices, makes implementation recommendations, and goes into detail about products and services. The framework aims to help you design your Google Cloud deployment so that it best matches your business needs. Seasoned experts created the framework at Google Cloud, including customer engineers, solution architects, cloud reliability engineers, and members of the professional service organization. Creating and managing Cloud Resources is one of the recommended initial quests for the Google Cloud learner - you will come in with little or no prior cloud knowledge, and come out with a practical experience that you can apply to your first Google Cloud project, From writing Cloud Shell commands and deploying your first virtual machine, to running applications on Kubernetes Engine or with load balancing.

This course introduces you to the essential concepts and terminologies used for working with the Google Cloud Platform. It doesn't only teach you but also helps you compare many of the computing and storage facilities available in the Google Cloud Platform, and this includes

Google cloud SQL, Google Kubernetes Engine, Google App Engine, Google Cloud Storage, Google Compute Engine. It will also teach you essential policy and resource management, including the Google Cloud Identity and Access Management, the Google Cloud Resource Manager Hierarchy. Amongst other courses, you'll be taught how to design and develop cloud-native applications that integrate managed services from the Google Cloud Platform. You'll be taught how to create repeatable deployments by treating infrastructure as code, choose the correct execution environment for a particular application and monitor application performance. All this will be done through a series of combinations of demos, hands-on lab and presentations. You are allowed to complete labs in your favourite language/code (Java, Python or Node J's). Through a combination of hands-on lab, demos and presentations, you'll learn how to apply the best practices for application development and use of appropriate GCP storage services for storing of objects, analytics, caching and relational data(you can do all this in our preferred language: Python or Java, Nodes.js). You'll be taught how to use GCP services and pre-trained machine learning APIs to build scalable, secure and intelligent cloud-native applications.

This course teaches you how to secure and also integrate the components of your application. Through a combination of hands-on lab, demos and presentations, you'll learn how to design and develop more secure applications, implement federated identity management and integrate your application components through the use of event-driven processing, API gateways and messaging (all these you can do in your favourite language/code - this is to enable you to finish as a professional).

You are introduced to the comprehensive, flexible infrastructure and platform services provided by Google Cloud with the focus on Compute Engine. You'll explore and deploy solution elements and infrastructure components such as networks and virtual machines, application services through a combination of demos, hands-on lab and presentations. Through the console and Cloud Shell, you'll learn how to use the Google Cloud. You'll also be taught the role of a cloud architect, the different approaches to infrastructure design and the virtual networking configuration, projects, network, subnetwork, up address and firewall rules. This course also covers deploying practical solutions including securely interconnecting networks, security and access management, customer-supplied encryption keys, quotas and billing, and resource monitoring.

The courses offered will cover a wide range of sections, including:

1. Plan and Design of a Cloud Solution Architecture

Design a solution infrastructure meeting business requirements

Design a solution infrastructure meeting technical requirements

Design storage, network, and compute resources

Create a migration plan

Envision of the solution improvements for future

2. Provision and Management of Solution Infrastructure

The configuration of network topologies

The configuration of individual storage systems

The configuration of computer systems

3. Compliance and Security Design

Design Security

Design legal compliance

4. Analysis and Optimization of business and technical processes

Analyze and define technical processes

Analyze and define business Processes

Develop procedures for testing solution resilience under production

5. Implementation Management

Advise operation/development and ensure that solution is implemented successfully

Read and write the languages for application development

6. Ensuring the reliability of solution and operations

Log, monitor, and alert solution

Release management and deployment

Support troubleshooting of operations

Evaluate different measures for quality control

To advance your preparation for the certification exam, we recommend you go through this material over and over again. Completing this foundational training can provide you with appropriate knowledge of Google's recommended best practices, thus bridging the technical knowledge gap. This training can improve your chance of success on the job you seek as well as certification assessment. Google certifications are an indicator of proficiency with their technology. Google Cloud certifications validate the expertise of individuals and show their ability to transform businesses with Google Cloud technology.

The Architecting with Google Kubernetes Engine specialization: This specialization as a whole will teach you how to implement solutions using Google Kubernetes Engine. In this course, Architecting with Google Kubernetes Engine, you'll learn how to build on your ability to Architect with GKE, and it includes hands-on labs for you to have a first-hand experience of its functionalities. You'll also learn how to define identity and access management roles as well as Kubernetes pod security policies. Unless you have successfully built an infrastructure for logging and monitoring, there will be no way to deliver a reliable and maintainable solution. Monitoring the application you designed will help you make decisions based on data rather than on just any impression. You'll also be introduced to use cases for a range of GCP managed storage services within Kubernetes applications. You could implement your storage systems, and that's a valid choice. But using managed services can get you into production faster, so they are worth your consideration. This course teaches individuals and organizations (operations team) the following skills:

- Understanding how software containers work
- Understanding the architecture of Kubernetes
- Understanding the architecture of Google Cloud Platform
- Understanding how pod networking works in Kubernetes Engine Create and manage Kubernetes Engine clusters using the GCP Console and cloud/ kubectl commands
- Launch, roll back and expose jobs in Kubernetes
- Manage access control using Kubernetes RBAC and Google Cloud IAM
- Managing pod security policies and network policies
- Using Secrets and ConfigMaps to isolate security credentials and configuration artifacts

- Understanding GCP choices for managed storage services monitor applications running in Kubernetes Engine.

This course also covers a section of the architecture framework, which explores how operational excellence results from efficiently running, managing and monitoring systems that deliver business value. Operational excellence helps you build a foundation for another critical principle, reliability.

To achieve operational excellence, use these strategies:

Automate build, test, and deploy.

Use continuous integration and continuous deployment (CI/CD) pipelines to build automated testing into your releases.

Perform automated integration testing and deployment.

Monitor business objectives metrics.

Define, measure, and alert on relevant business metrics.

Conduct disaster recovery testing.

Don't wait for a disaster to strike. Instead, periodically verify that your disaster recovery procedures work and test the processes regularly. Some best practices taught are:

- Increase software development and release velocity.
- Monitor for system health and business health.
- Plan and design for failures.

Increase development and release velocity

Use a CI/CD approach to increase velocity. First, you make your software development team more productive and automate integration testing into the build process. You automate deployment after your build meets your specific testing criteria. Your developers can make smaller and more frequent changes. The changes are thoroughly tested, and the time to deploy them is reduced.

You can choose how your application is rolled out. It's a best practice to do canary testing and observe your system for any errors, which is easier if you have a robust monitoring and alerting system. In Google Cloud, you can use managed instance groups (MIGs) to do A/B or canary testing, as well as to perform a slow rollout or a rollback if required.

Design questions

How does your development team manage to build and release?

What integration and security testing does your development team employ?

How do you roll back?

Recommendations

Make the CI/CD pipeline the only way to deploy to production.

Isolate and secure your CI/CD environment.

Build only once and promote the result through the pipeline.

Keep your CI/CD pipelines fast.

Minimize branching in your version control system.

Key services

Cloud Source Repositories is a fully-featured, private Git repository service hosted on Google Cloud. You can use Cloud Source Repositories for collaborative development of any application or service.

Container Registry is a single place for your team to manage Docker images, perform vulnerability analysis, and decide who can access what with fine-grained access control. Existing CI/CD integrations allow you to set up fully automated Docker pipelines to get fast feedback.

Cloud Build is a service that executes your builds on the Google Cloud infrastructure. Cloud Build can import source code from GitHub, Bitbucket, Cloud Storage, or Cloud Source Repositories, perform a build to your specifications, and produce artifacts such as Docker containers or Java archives.

The DevOps Resource and Assessment (DORA) project defines monitoring as follows: Monitoring is the process of collecting, analyzing, and using the information to track applications and infrastructure to guide business decisions. Monitoring is a crucial capability because it gives you insight into your systems and your work. Through monitoring, you can make decisions about the impact of changes to your service, apply the scientific method to incident response, and measure your service's alignment with your business goals. With monitoring in place, you can do the following:

- Analyze long-term trends.
- Compare your experiments over time.
- Define alerting on critical metrics.
- Build relevant real-time dashboards.
- Perform retrospective analysis.

Monitor both business-driven metrics and system health metrics. Business-driven metrics help you understand how well your systems support your business. For example, you could follow the cost to serve a user in an application, the change in volume of traffic to your site following a redesign, or how long it takes a customer to purchase a product on your website. System health metrics help you understand whether your systems are operating correctly and within acceptable performance levels.

Use the following four golden signals to monitor your system:

Latency: This is defined as the time the system takes to respond to a request

Traffic: This is defined as the amount of demand placed on your system.

Errors: The rate of requests that fail. Requests can fail explicitly (for example, HTTP 500s), implicitly (for example, an HTTP 200 success response, but with the wrong content), or by policy (for example, if you committed to one-second response times, any request that takes more than one second is an error).

Saturation speaks of how full your service is. A measure of your most constrained resources. (That is, in a memory-constrained system, show memory; in an I/O-constrained system, show I/O).

Logging

Logging services are critical to monitoring your systems. While metrics form the basis of specific items to track, logs contain valuable information that you need for debugging, security-related analysis and for compliance requirements. Google Cloud includes Cloud Logging, an integrated logging service you can use to store, search, analyze, monitor, and alert on log data and events from Google Cloud. Cloud Logging automatically collects logs from Google Cloud services. You can use these logs to build metrics for monitoring and to create logging exports to external services such as Cloud Storage, BigQuery, and Pub/Sub.

Design for disaster recovery

Designing your system to anticipate and handle failure scenarios helps ensure that if there is a catastrophe, the impact on your systems is minimized. To expect failures, make sure you have a well-defined and regularly tested disaster recovery (DR) plan to back up and restore services and data. Service-interrupting events (events that affect the services delivered) can happen at any time. Your network could have an outage, your latest application push might introduce a critical bug, or you might have to contend with a natural disaster. When things go awry, it's essential to have a robust, targeted, and well-tested DR plan.

CONCLUSION/ APPRECIATION

We sincerely appreciate your purchase of our book that reveals useful information about everything you need to know about Google Professional Cloud Architect. We hope you loved it.

Thanks,

Jason Hoffman.